GASB Statement No. 34

Implementation Recommendations for School Districts

2nd Edition

Gary Heinfeld

Published in partnership with the
Association of School Business Officials International

SCARECROWEDUCATION
Lanham, Maryland • Toronto • Oxford
2003

KH

Published in partnership with
the Association of School Business Officials International

Published in the United States of America
by ScarecrowEducation
An imprint of The Rowman & Littlefield Publishing Group, Inc.
4501 Forbes Boulevard, Suite 200, Lanham, Maryland 20706
www.scarecroweducation.com

PO Box 317
Oxford
OX2 9RU, UK

British Library Cataloguing in Publication Information Available

Library of Congress Cataloging-in-Publication Data

Heinfeld, Gary.
    GASB statement no. 34, implementation recommendations for school districts / Gary
Heinfeld.—2nd ed.
        p.   cm.
    "Published in partnership with the Association of School Business Officials
International."
    ISBN 1-57886-045-8 (pbk. : alk. paper)
    1. School districts—United States—Finance.   2. Financial statements—United
States.   I. Title: Implementation recommendations for school districts.
II. Association of School Business Officials International.   III. Title.
LB2830.2 .H45   2003
371.2'06'0973—dc22   2003017026

10/25/04

ASBO International
Accounting, Auditing and Budgeting Committee
Sub-Committee on GASB Statement No. 34 Implementation

Nicholas C. A. Alioto, CPA
Assistant Superintendent of Business
Kenosha Unified School District No 1
Kenosha, Wisconsin
nalioto@kusd.edu

Denny G. Bolton, Ph.D., RSBA
Business Administrator / Board Secretary
Owen J. Roberts School District
Pottstown, Pennsylvania
DBolton@ojr.k12.pa.us

E. Danny Cash, RSBA
Assistant Superintendent—Finance and
Operations
Community Consolidated School District 21
Wheeling, Illinois
dcash@d21.k12.il.us

Roger J. Dickson, RSBA
Assistant Superintendent for Business
Kettle Moraine School District
Wales, Wisconsin
roger@kmsd.edu

Gary Heinfeld, CPA, CGFM
Managing Partner
Heinfeld, Meech & Co., P.C. CPA's
Tucson, Arizona
gary@heinfeldmeech.com

George M. Lingel
Assistant Superintendent for Business
Community Consolidated School District 15
Palatine, Illinois
lingelg@esc.ccsd15.k12.il.us

Jack W. McKelvy, RSBA
Executive Director of Support Services
Mesa County School District #51
Grand Junction, Colorado
JMcKelvy@mesa.k12.co.us

ASBO Staff Liaison

Linda Prevatte
Director of Professional Development

Technical Editors

Edward Blaha
Deputy Director
Georgia Department of Audits and Accounts
Atlanta, Georgia
blahaef@audits.state.ga.us

Tim Green, CPA
Partner
Allen, Green & Company, LLP
Monroe, Louisiana
tim@allengreencpa.com

W. Gary Harmer, CPA
Assistant Superintendent of Business Services
Salt Lake City School District
Salt Lake City, Utah
Gark.harmer@slc.k12.ut.us

George Scott
Partner
Deloitte & Touche, LLP
Fort Worth, Texas
gscott@dttus.com

ASBO would like to acknowledge and express its appreciation to the GASB staff, particularly David Bean, Randy Finden, Dean Mead and Ken Schermann, for assisting us in editing this Guide and providing their technical assistance and advice. In addition, we would like to acknowledge the assistance of Mark Hessel of VRM-MAXIMUS in developing the Asset Life Figure.

Contents

Introduction

After more than ten years of deliberation and debate with substantial controversy and compromise along the way, the Governmental Accounting Standards Board (GASB) on June 30, 1999, unanimously approved GASB Statement No. 34, *Basic Financial Statements—and Management's Discussion and Analysis—for State and Local Governments*. Statement 34 is arguably the most significant change in the history of governmental accounting. It is a dramatic change in the way that school districts report and present financial information. The new reporting model affects every school organization that issues financial statements in conformity with Generally Accepted Accounting Principles (GAAP).

The term *reporting model* is used in this publication to describe the minimum set of financial statements, note disclosures, and required supplementary information (RSI) that must be presented in a financial report for an independent auditor to assert, without qualification or further comment, that a government's financial statements are fairly presented in conformity with GAAP. The financial statements and the accompanying notes are the focus of the independent audit. However, the independent auditor is required to perform certain limited procedures in connection with RSI, such as making inquiries of management regarding RSI measurement and presentation.

The current financial reporting model for school districts has existed for most of the twentieth century. The National Council on Governmental Accounting (NCGA) provided a definitive form to the model with the publication of NCGA Statement 1, *Governmental Accounting and Financial Reporting Principles* in 1979. Statement 1 contributed significantly to the standardization and enhancement of accounting and financial reporting. However, during the past several years, there has been an emerging consensus regarding the need for governmental entities to institute financial reporting that promotes improved fiscal and operational accountability. This consensus stimulated the GASB to commence a comprehensive evaluation of the traditional financial reporting model. This effort eventually resulted in Statement 34 and the establishment of a new governmental financial reporting model.

There are two separate and equally important aspects of accountability. The understanding of these two components is critical to the rationale for the enhancements in Statement 34 to the traditional financial reporting model. First, fiscal accountability requires that districts demonstrate compliance with public decisions concerning the raising and spending of public monies in the short term, which is usually a single budgetary cycle or one year. Second, operational accountability requires that a district demonstrate the extent to which it has met and can continue to meet its operating objectives in an efficient and effective manner.

The traditional financial reporting model has a strong emphasis on legal compliance as a means to promote fiscal accountability with only minor attention to operational accountability. Statement 34 will improve operational accountability by highlighting the district-wide perspective that was frequently lost in the detail of fund accounting. Figure I-1 presents a summary comparison of the key improvements in fiscal and operational accountability of the new governmental financial reporting model.

While Statement 34 includes significant requirements that enhance financial reporting, it does not abandon the traditional public-sector approach to accounting and fiscal disclosure. Rather, GASB has integrated many of the most popular features of traditional financial reporting into the new model.

The requirements in Statement 34 are also designed to make annual reports easier to understand for the public and more useful to stakeholders who utilize the financial information, such as investors and creditors. The new standards represent a substantial advance in the disclosure of more meaningful and useful financial information by school districts.

Specifically, Statement 34 establishes new requirements for the annual financial report of school districts. Figure I-2 provides the basic frame-

Figure I-1　Key Changes to Fiscal and Operational Accountability.

Changes to Enhance Fiscal Accountability		*Changes to Enhance Operational Accountability*	
Previous Model	*New Model*	*Previous Model*	*New Model*
Information in basic financial statements aggregated by fund type	Information in basic financial statements presented separately for major governmental and enterprise funds	All reporting based on fund and fund types	Introduction of district-wide financial statements
Budgetary comparisons associated with the basic financial statements aggregated by fund type	Budgetary comparisons associated with the basic financial statements presented for the general fund and each major special revenue fund with a legally adopted budget	Information on governmental activities limited to near-term inflows and outflows of spendable resources	District-wide financial statements provide additional long-term focus for governmental activities
Budgetary comparisons report only final amended budget	Budgetary comparisons report both original and final amended budget	Cost data available for business-type activities	Cost data provided for both governmental and business-type activities
		No narrative required	Narrative overview and analysis required in the form of Management's Discussion and Analysis

work of the new model for the presentation of the annual financial report. The most important features of the model are:

- *Government-wide financial reporting*
  Districts will be required to produce financial reports that provide a clear picture of the organization as a single, unified entity. These new "district-wide" financial statements complement rather than replace tradi-

Figure I-2   New Financial Reporting Model: Minimum Information Required for Fair Presentation in Conformity with Generally Accepted Accounting Principles (GAAP).

Management's Discussion and Analysis

District-Wide Financial Statements
Statement of Net Assets
Statement of Activities

Fund Financial Statements
Governmental Funds:
Balance Sheet
Statement of Revenues, Expenditures and Changes in Fund Balances
Proprietary Funds:
Statement of Net Assets
Statement of Revenues, Expenses and Changes in Net Assets
Statement of Cash Flows
Fiduciary Funds:
Statement of Fiduciary Net Assets
Statement of Changes in Fiduciary Net Assets (not applicable to agency funds)

Notes to the Financial Statements

Other Required Supplementary Information
Budgetary Comparison Schedules
Infrastructure assets reported using the modified approach (if any)

tional fund-based financial statements. (We will refer to the government-wide statements as district-wide statements throughout this Guide.)

- *Additional long-term focus for school activities*
  Traditional reporting for tax-supported activities has focused on short-term inflows, outflows, and balances of available financial resources. The new financial reporting model retains this short-term focus in the governmental fund financial statements while providing a long-term perspective for these same activities in the district-wide financial statements.

- *Narrative overview and analysis*
  The new model provides those who use financial reports with a narrative introduction, overview, and analysis of the basic financial statements in the form of management's discussion and analysis (MD&A).

- *Information on major funds*
  There is a general consensus that fund information is most useful when presented for individual funds rather than when funds are combined, such as the aggregation of special revenue funds. Accordingly, the new financial reporting model requires the presentation of individual fund data for each of the major funds of the school district.
- *Expanded budgetary reporting*
  In the past, budgetary comparisons were based solely on the final amended budget. Under the new model, information on the original budget must also be presented. In addition, the new model eliminates aggregated budget presentations in favor of comparisons for the general fund and each major special revenue fund with an annual legally adopted budget.

Statement 34 is primarily based on GASB Concepts Statement No. 1, *Objectives of Financial Reporting*, published in 1987. Some of the objectives in Statement No. 1 affirmed the importance of the financial information that districts currently include in their annual reports. In addition, Statement No. 1 advocated new standards for financial reporting that move districts closer to the accounting standards for private-sector businesses. Statement 34 meets the objectives of Statement No. 1 by requiring districts to retain much of the current information in their annual reports, in addition to the presentation of new and different financial data. Among the major innovations of Statement 34, districts will be required to:

- Provide information about the cost of delivering services to students.
- Include for the first time information about general infrastructure assets of the school district, if any.

To help school business officials implement the changes in Statement 34, the Association of School Business Officials (ASBO) International has published these implementation recommendations. These recommendations have been prepared by the Accounting, Auditing, and Budgeting Committee: Subcommittee on GASB Statement 34 Implementation.

This document presents the new standards and provides examples of the required financial reports. It is supplemented with information in three appendices. The first appendix is the illustrative MD&A provided by

GASB in its school district user guide. The second appendix presents a school district's actual MD&A. The third appendix discusses the impact of Statement 34 on the preparation of a Comprehensive Annual Financial Report (CAFR) based on the requirements of the Certificate of Excellence (COE) program of ASBO International.

This introduction will provide a brief review of the GASB, summarize the implementation schedule for the new reporting standards, and present an overview of the chapters in the Implementation Guide for Statement 34.

GOVERNMENTAL ACCOUNTING STANDARDS BOARD (GASB)

GASB was formed in 1984 to develop and improve financial reporting rules for the more than 84,000 state and local governments in the United States, including school districts. It operates under the auspices of the not-for-profit Financial Accounting Foundation, which oversees and appoints the members of the GASB, as well as the Financial Accounting Standards Board (the FASB). The GASB is not part of any government. Adhering to its pronouncements is required in most states. GASB pronouncements must be followed when a state or local government's audit report states that it follows generally accepted accounting principles, or GAAP. Bond covenants associated with the issuance of debt often require school districts to follow GAAP.

IMPLEMENTATION OF STATEMENT 34

School districts must prepare financial statements in accordance with the new standards in three phases, depending on the total revenues of the district in its first fiscal year ending after June 15, 1999. *Phase One* school districts with annual revenues of $100 million or more must comply with Statement 34 for fiscal years beginning after June 15, 2001. *Phase Two* school districts with annual revenues of $10 million or more and less than $100 million must comply for fiscal years beginning after June 15, 2002. *Phase Three* school districts with annual revenues under $10 million must comply for fiscal years beginning after June 15, 2003. Figure I-3 provides more detail on the implementation schedule.

Figure I-3   Timetable for Implementing the New Financial Reporting Model.

Size of government	All provisions except retroactive reporting of major general infrastructure assets (if any)	Retroactive reporting of major general infrastructure assets
$100 million or more total annual revenues*	Years beginning after 06-15-01**	Years beginning after 06-15-05
Less than $100 million but ≥ $10 million total annual revenues*	Years beginning after 06-15-02**	Years beginning after 06-15-06
Less than $10 million total annual revenues*	Years beginning after 06-15-03**	Optional

*For this purpose, "total revenues" are those of the school district's governmental and enterprise funds in the first fiscal year ending after June 15, 1999, excluding extraordinary items.
**GASB 34 paragraph 142 requires component units to early implement if the primary government chooses early implementation. Accordingly, school districts that are component units must monitor the primary government's implementation timeline in order to comply with GASB 34.

STATEMENT 34 IMPLEMENTATION RECOMMENDATIONS

This document is divided into eight chapters addressing Statement 34 implementation recommendations. Many of the financial illustrations and statements in this guide have been adapted from the school district user guide published by GASB. In addition, GASB has published two implementation guides titled *Guide to Implementation of GASB Statement 34 on Basic Financial Statements—and Management's Discussion and Anal-*

ysis—for State and Local Governments and *Guide to Implementation of GASB Statement 34 on Basic Financial Statements—and Management's Discussion and Analysis—for State and Local Governments—Second Question and Answer.* GASB's implementation guides are presented in a question-and-answer format. Both of the GASB publications are useful resources for business officials to utilize when preparing financial statements in conformance with the new reporting model.

ASBO's implementation recommendations are specific to school districts while the GASB implementation guides are for all types of state and local governments. ASBO's implementation recommendations are cross-referenced to specific questions in GASB's first implementation guide. The references are enclosed within parenthesis throughout the text. For example, (Q105–106) refers the reader to questions and answers 105 and 106 in GASB's implementation guide. ASBO's implementation recommendations include specific guidance to meeting the requirements of Statement 34, where GASB has allowed multiple methods. ASBO believes school districts will achieve greater comparability and uniformity in financial reporting if districts apply the new standards using the same methodology.

Following is a summary of each chapter's contents.

MANAGEMENT'S DISCUSSION & ANALYSIS (CHAPTER ONE)

One of Statement 34's new requirements is that a school district must include a new presentation referred to as Management's Discussion and Analysis (MD&A), which is required supplementary information (RSI). The MD&A is required to precede the basic financial statements and notes. The MD&A is intended to be an easily readable and objective analysis of the school district's financial activities. It will introduce the financial statements and provide the reader with an analysis of the district's financial activities.

The MD&A will provide an analysis of the school district's overall financial position and operating results. Its purpose is to help users of the financial statements to assess if the district's financial position has improved or deteriorated. The analysis must include a comparison of the current year to the prior year based on the district-wide financial information about assets, liabilities, revenues, and expenses. In addition, the analysis will explain significant variations in fund-based financial results and budgetary information and will describe capital asset and long-term debt activity during the year. The MD&A will include a description of currently known facts, decisions, or conditions expected to have a significant effect on the future financial position and results of operations of the school district.

DISTRICT-WIDE FINANCIAL STATEMENTS
(CHAPTER TWO)

The new basic financial statements will be composed of district-wide financial statements, fund financial statements, and notes to the financial statements. Perhaps the most notable feature of the new model is the requirement for district-wide financial statements. The focus is on the school district as a whole rather than on individual funds. The district-wide statements must be prepared on an accrual basis of accounting for all of the activities of the district. Under the accrual basis, all revenues and costs of providing services are reported, not just those received or paid in the current year or soon thereafter. This approach moves governmental accounting closer to financial reporting in the private sector.

The district-wide financial statements must be prepared on an economic resources measurement focus, which includes all of a school district's resources, both capital and financial, current and long term. The statements would therefore include current assets, capital assets, current liabilities, and long-term liabilities. The district-wide financial statements consist of two statements:

- A statement of net assets (equivalent to a balance sheet): The statement of net assets is used to report all that a school district owns (assets) and owes (liabilities). A school district's assets include financial resources such as cash, receivables, and investments. Capital assets, such as equipment, land, and buildings, are included in the statement. Liabilities include amounts owed to vendors (payables) and various debt instruments such as bonds, notes and leases as well as obligations incurred in connection with district operations such as salaries payable, unused vacation leave, claims, and judgments.
- A statement of activities (equivalent to an income statement): The

statement of activities is used to report all changes in a district's net assets. This statement focuses on expenses (costs) rather than expenditures (near-term outflows of spendable resources). Expenses include depreciation on capital assets.

Each of the district-wide statements must distinguish between the governmental and business-type activities of the primary government and its discretely presented component units by reporting each in separate columns. Fiduciary activities, whose resources are not available to finance school programs, are excluded from the district-wide statements.

FUND FINANCIAL STATEMENTS
(CHAPTER THREE)

Until now, annual reports have divided financial information among a variety of funds. These funds have been established by governing bodies such as federal and state departments of education, state legislatures, or school districts. Such an approach facilitated the control of resources and permitted measurement, in the short term, of the revenues and expenditures arising from a particular activity. Because the users of financial information continue to assess compliance with finance-related laws, rules, and regulations, Statement 34 requires districts to continue to present financial statements with information about funds.

The focus of these fund-based statements has been sharpened, however, by requiring districts to report information about their most important or *major* funds, including the school district's general fund. Until now, fund information has been reported in the aggregate by type of fund, which obscures individual funds. This often makes it difficult to assess a district's accountability for a significant individual program or particular dedicated revenue.

Another important objective of annual reports is to provide a comparison of the inflows of the resources of a district with its outflows. Statements for governmental funds will continue to use the flow of current financial resources measurement focus. These statements will show the short-term performance of individual funds using the same measures that most districts use to manage their resources. This is in contrast to the long-term focus of accrual-based district-wide statements.

Districts will continue to provide budgetary comparison information in their annual reports. An important change, however, is a requirement to add the district's original budget to the current comparison of final budget-to-actual results. Many school districts revise their original budgets over the course of the year for a variety of reasons. The reporting of the original budget adds a new analytical dimension and increases the usefulness of the budgetary comparison. It will facilitate some assessment on how accurately a district can estimate and manage its general resources.

CAPITAL ASSETS AND DEPRECIATION
(CHAPTER FOUR)

Statement 34 requires capitalization and depreciation of all exhaustible capital assets, including infrastructure (if any) assets, in the district-wide financial statements. Capital assets (equipment, land, and buildings) are less easily converted to cash and less spendable than financial assets (cash, receivables, and investments). Infrastructure assets, such as roads and bridges, are long-lived capital assets that are normally stationary in nature and normally can be preserved for a significantly greater number of years than most capital assets. Most school districts will not have significant infrastructure assets. All school districts must now capitalize and depreciate exhaustible capital assets. School districts that have infrastructure assets should refer to Statement 34 and the GASB implementation guides for assistance in meeting reporting requirements.

NOTES TO THE FINANCIAL STATEMENTS
(CHAPTER FIVE)

The notes to the financial statements provide additional information that is essential for the statements to fairly represent the school district's financial position. The notes contain important information that is not part of the financial statements. However, the notes are an integral part of the statements, not an appendage to them. Statement 34 requires changes to disclosures in the notes to the financial statements for summary of significant accounting policies, capital assets, and long-term debt. Further, the notes to the financial statements may include certain detail disclosures to reconcile the differences between district-wide and fund financial statements.

THE COMPREHENSIVE ANNUAL FINANCIAL REPORT (CHAPTER SIX)

Many districts publish their annual financial reports as part of a larger comprehensive annual financial report (CAFR). The CAFR contains additional financial, economic, and demographic information that is useful in the analysis of the school district's financial position and operational results.

Statement 34 does not change the CAFR's basic framework, which includes an introductory section, a financial section, and a statistical section. However, the financial section must now include the MD&A, basic financial statements and other RSI as well as combining and individual nonmajor fund statements and schedules.

ACHIEVING EXCELLENCE WITH FINANCIAL REPORTING (CHAPTER SEVEN)

A critical tool for the implementation of Statement 34 is a report writer. Various spreadsheet programs are great for single page reports; however, a database system is the way to go to save time and ensure reliable reports for financial statements. When selecting a report writer, you should consider one that can produce current model reports as well as Statement 34 reports. This ability will become important during the implementation of Statement 34, as you will need to convert your last year's current model financial statements to Statement 34 financial statements.

GAO NEW INDEPENDENCE STANDARD (CHAPTER EIGHT)

This chapter covers what the auditors can or cannot do for the audit client. In certain circumstances it is not appropriate for audit organizations to perform both audit and selected non-audit services for the same client.

For more information on financial reporting and financial statement examples under Statement 34, order another guide from ASBO International entitled *Financial Reporting under GASB Statement No. 34*. This guide presents two complete Comprehensive Annual Financial Reports (CAFR's), one under the old reporting model and one under GASB Statement No. 34.

Chapter One

Management's Discussion and Analysis

This chapter provides guidance and suggestions for the Management's Discussion and Analysis (MD&A), a new requirement of Statement 34. The MD&A is intended to give the reader an easy-to-understand overview of the school district's financial position and results of operations for the year. Management is also required to explain why the district's financial position has improved, deteriorated, or remained the same when compared with the prior year. The analysis is to be based only on *currently* known facts as of the date of the auditor's report. Discussion of anticipated future developments or events is not permitted in the MD&A. The MD&A precedes and introduces the financial statements.

If the school district prepares a comprehensive annual financial report (CAFR), the MD&A does not replace the transmittal letter. The transmittal letter will still introduce the CAFR and as such will precede the MD&A (Q6). The transmittal letter should not replicate information contained in the MD&A. The transmittal letter may discuss anticipated events, which are specifically excluded from the MD&A. For more information as to the effects of Statement 34 on the CAFR, refer to Chapter Six of this Guide.

The MD&A is required supplementary information (RSI). As such, the auditor must perform certain limited procedures and report any deficiencies or omissions.

Statement 34, paragraphs 6a and 8 through 11, includes the specific elements of MD&A (Q10). The information that follows is a summary of those elements with suggestions and examples.

1

1. Although the MD&A is RSI, it is required to precede the basic financial statements. It is designed to give the reader an objective and easily readable analysis of the school district's overall financial activities.
2. The MD&A is management's responsibility. The analysis and associated information and conclusions are to be based on known developments and occurrences as of the date of the auditor's report. "What if" or information about potential developments or future planned events is not considered to be currently known facts and should not be included in the MD&A.
3. The MD&A should emphasize current-year results in comparison with the prior year. In the year of implementation, prior year data is not required, but is encouraged.
4. Districts are encouraged to include charts, graphs, and tables to enhance readers' understanding. These tools should be used to enhance rather than replace required presentations of financial data.
5. Discussion and analysis should focus on the primary government; however consideration should be given to component units based on their size and the relationship with the primary government.
6. The MD&A will discuss the basic financial statements, which include the district-wide and fund financial statements. The MD&A should help the reader understand the differences and how the statements complement each other. The narrative should describe the measurement focus and bases of accounting of both sets of financial statements (Q11). In the year of implementation, the school district should explain that the district-wide financial statements are new and have not been required or provided in the past. The school district should provide a description of the two new statements, the statement of net assets and the statement of activities, and what they are intended to report.
7. In the MD&A, school districts are required to analyze data reported in the financial statements and give appropriate explanations for significant changes that took place during the period.
8. Condensed financial information, derived from district-wide statements, with explanations of significant changes between the current and prior year is required in the MD&A. The MD&A will

include information needed to support analysis of financial position and results of operation. The following elements, at a minimum, should be included in condensed information (Q12):

a. Total assets, distinguishing between capital and other assets
b. Total liabilities, distinguishing between long-term liabilities and other liabilities
c. Total net assets, distinguishing among amounts invested in capital assets, net of related debt; restricted amounts; and unrestricted amounts
d. Program revenues by major source
e. General revenues by major source
f. Total revenues
g. Program expenses, at a minimum by function
h. Total expenses
i. Excess (deficiency) before contributions to term and permanent endowments or permanent fund principal, special and extraordinary items, and transfers
j. Contributions
k. Special and extraordinary items
l. Transfers
m. Change in net assets
n. Ending net assets

9. The analysis of financial position and results of operations in the MD&A should help the user answer the questions listed below. The analysis should be factual, reliable and understandable.

- Did the school district's overall financial position improve or decline from the prior year?
- Did the school district earn enough revenues during the year to cover expenses incurred during the year (did revenues equal or exceed expenses)?
- Did the school district report what it cost for services delivered?
- Did the school district generate a portion of service costs by user fees, grants, etc., or were tax revenues used to cover the cost of services?
- Did the school district's investment in capital assets change?

Figure 1-1, following, is an example of a condensed schedule of net assets for a school district. It provides a summary of the school

Chapter One

Figure 1-1   Condensed Schedule of Net Assets (in Millions of Dollars).

	Governmental Activities		Business-type Activities		Total School District		Percentage Change
	2001	2002	2001	2002	2001	2002	2001-2002
Current and other assets	$ 117.8	$ 142.8	$ 9.9	$ 11.2	$ 127.7	$ 154.0	20.6%
Capital assets	329.1	315.5	1.9	2.5	331.0	318.1	-3.9%
Total assets	**446.9**	**458.4**	**11.8**	**13.7**	**458.7**	**472.1**	**2.9%**
Long-term debt	134.0	118.8	-	-	134.0	118.8	-11.3%
Other liabilities	40.4	48.0	0.7	1.3	41.1	49.3	20.0%
Total liabilities	**174.4**	**166.8**	**0.7**	**1.3**	**175.1**	**168.1**	**-4.0%**
Net assets							
Invested in capital assets,							
net of related debt	219.2	231.1	1.9	2.5	221.1	233.7	5.7%
Restricted	6.0	5.5	-	-	6.0	5.5	-7.5%
Unrestricted	47.3	54.9	9.2	9.9	56.6	64.8	14.5%
Total net assets	**$ 272.5**	**$ 291.6**	**$ 11.1**	**$ 12.4**	**$ 283.6**	**$ 304.0**	**7.2%**

Note: totals may not add due to rounding.

district's net assets for the fiscal year ending in 2001 compared with 2002. An accompanying narrative should be included to explain the significant changes, such as growth in current assets, the change in capital assets, why liabilities varied from one year to the next, and the change in restricted assets.

Figure 1-2 illustrates the impact that results of operations had on changes in net assets in the fiscal year ending 2001 and 2002. Like the previous figure, the condensed schedule of changes in net assets should include a narrative explaining significant changes.

Figure 1-3 is an example of a condensed schedule showing the net cost of governmental activities. (This schedule exceeds GASB's minimum requirement by also presenting the total cost of services, but its inclusion is recommended by ASBO.) The net cost of services is the result after subtracting grants and charges for services that the district used to offset the program's total cost.

10. The MD&A should include an analysis of balances and transactions of individual funds. The analysis needs to identify reasons for significant changes in fund balances or fund net assets and explain any restrictions, commitments, or other limitations affecting fund resources availability for future uses.

   • Management should discuss the change in fund balance(s) from the prior year for the district's major funds. Management is required to explain the reason(s) for any significant changes. An

Figure 1-2 Changes in Net Assets from Operating Results (in Millions of Dollars).

	Governmental Activities		Business-type Activities		Total School District		Total Percentage Change
	2001	2002	2001	2002	2001	2002	2001-2002
Revenues							
Program revenues							
Charges for services	$ 7.9	$ 8.5	$ 5.0	$ 5.7	$ 12.9	$ 14.2	10.2%
Operating Grants & Contributions	38.3	42.3	15.3	17.0	53.7	59.3	10.4%
Capital Grants & Contributions				0.7	-	0.7	
General revenues							
Property taxes	162.8	171.0	-	-	162.8	171.0	5.0%
State formula aid	175.0	176.3	-	-	175.0	176.3	0.7%
Other	6.8	7.4	0.3	0.3	7.0	7.7	9.5%
Total revenues	**390.8**	**405.4**	**20.6**	**23.7**	**411.4**	**429.1**	**4.3%**
Expenses							
Instruction	228.9	234.8			228.9	234.8	2.6%
Pupil & Instructional Services	44.8	44.0			44.8	44.0	-1.8%
Administration & Business	43.7	41.4			43.7	41.4	-5.3%
Maintenance & operations	29.5	30.4			29.5	30.4	3.1%
Transportation	8.8	8.6			8.8	8.6	-2.3%
Other	23.4	28.5	20.2	22.4	43.6	50.9	16.7%
Total expenses	**379.1**	**387.7**	**20.2**	**22.4**	**399.3**	**410.1**	**2.7%**
Excess (deficiency) before special item	11.7	17.7	0.4	1.3	12.1	19.0	56.9%
Special item: land sale	-	1.4	-	-	-	1.4	-
Increase (decrease) in net assets	**$ 11.7**	**$ 19.1**	**$ 0.4**	**$ 1.3**	**$ 12.1**	**$ 20.4**	**68.2%**

Note: totals may not add due to rounding.

overview of changes in revenues and expenditures is appropriate. This would include an explanation of both financial (reasons for major revenue adjustments and program expenditure adjustments) and non-financial (board/district philosophy or legislative changes that affected fund balances) changes. The reasons and explanation for changes would be based on the individual circumstances of the district.

Additional discussion is required to inform the reader of any commitments or obligations that have been placed on fund resources that limits their use in the future.

11. All school districts are required to include budgetary comparison schedules or statements either as RSI or as part of the basic financial statements for the general fund and each major special revenue fund with a legally adopted budget. The school district should include in the MD&A an explanation of significant differences

Figure 1-3   Net Cost of Governmental Activities (in Millions of Dollars).

	Total Cost of Services		Percentage Change	Net Cost of Services		Percentage Change
	2001	2002	2001-2002	2001	2002	2001-2002
Instruction	$ 228.9	$ 234.8	2.6%	$ 197.3	$ 201.6	2.2%
Pupil & Instructional Services	$ 44.8	$ 44.0	-1.8%	36.3	36.1	-0.6%
Administration & Business	$ 43.7	$ 41.4	-5.3%	39.2	36.8	-6.1%
Maintenance & operations	$ 29.5	$ 30.4	3.1%	26.7	27.5	3.0%
Transportation	$ 8.8	$ 8.6	-2.3%	7.6	7.8	2.6%
Other	$ 23.4	$ 28.5	21.8%	25.7	27.1	5.4%
Total	**$ 379.1**	**$ 387.7**	**2.3%**	**$ 332.8**	**$ 336.9**	**1.2%**

Note: totals may not add due to rounding.

between the original and final budget amounts and between final budget amounts and actual budget results for the general fund. The explanation(s) should be specific to the events that took place, such as higher/lower cost of opening/expanding/closing facilities, change in student count/growth, program changes, change in staff or staffing patterns, revenue flow, etc.

12. The MD&A should include a description of significant capital asset and long-term debt activity that occurred during the year. The discussion needs to reveal commitments for capital expenditures, changes in credit rating, and debt limitations that may affect financing of planned facilities or services. Again, this discussion should be limited to events that have taken place, not anticipated future events.

   • The notes to the financial statements require certain disclosure for capital assets and long-term liabilities. The requirement for the MD&A is to summarize the information and give additional information to explain the difference between years. Additionally, it would be appropriate to include data on legal margin of indebtedness.

   • Figure 1-4, illustrates capital assets, net of depreciation, by asset type. Management would need to explain the reason(s) for significant changes.

   • Figure 1-5 illustrates a condensed summary of outstanding long-term debt. Management should explain the reason(s) for such changes.

13. Statement 34 requires districts that use the modified approach to

Figure 1-4   Capital Assets (Net of Depreciation, in Millions of Dollars).

	Governmental Activities		Business-type Activities		Total School District		Total Percentage Change
	2001	2002	2001	2002	2001	2002	2001-2002
Land	$ 22.1	$ 20.8	-	-	$ 22.1	$ 20.8	-5.6%
Construction in progress	11.4	11.4	-	-	11.4	11.4	0.4%
Buildings	188.5	177.9	-	-	188.5	177.9	-5.7%
Equipment & furniture	106.9	105.4	$ 1.9	$ 2.5	108.8	107.9	-0.9%
Total	$ 329.0	$ 315.5	$ 1.9	$ 2.5	$ 330.9	$ 318.1	-3.9%

Note: totals may not add due to rounding.

report some or all of their infrastructure assets to discuss significant changes in assessed condition, how the current assessed condition compares with the condition level the district has established, and any significant differences from the estimated annual amount to maintain or preserve infrastructure assets compared with actual amounts spent during the current year. Infrastructure (roads, bridges, water and sewer systems, etc.) is generally not a major issue for school districts. Consequently this guide does not cover infrastructure assets.

14. In addition to specific required information, the MD&A should include any other currently known facts that are expected to have a significant effect on the district's financial position or results of operation. It is management's responsibility to identify these changes and inform the readers so they may be aware of the potential impact to the district. For MD&A purposes, currently known

Figure 1-5   Outstanding Long-Term Debt (in Millions of Dollars).

	Total School District		Total Percentage Change
	2001	2002	2001-2002
General obligation bonds & notes (financed with property taxes)	$ 108.2	$ 96.5	-10.8%
Other general obligation debt	5.8	4.7	-19.0%
Total	$ 114.0	$ 101.2	-11.2%

facts are as of the date of the auditor's report (Q13–14). Examples include:

- changes in legislation regarding school finance;
- approved capital projects;
- major commercial development expected to affect the tax base;
- major residential development expected to affect student enrollment;
- litigation that has been concluded;
- approved debt that has not had an impact, as of yet, on the school district's overall financial condition; and
- award and acceptance of a major grant.

Chapter Two

District-Wide Financial Statements

Statement 34 requires the preparation of *district-wide* financial statements as an element of the basic financial statements (Q4). School districts must present a statement of net assets and a statement of activities. The district-wide statements present aggregated financial information using the accrual basis of accounting. Fiduciary funds are not included in this aggregated format. The new district-wide financial statements (i.e., Statement of Net Assets and Statement of Activities) moves the school district closer to the accounting standards for private-sector businesses.

Statement 34 allows some flexibility as to presentation of the new statements, particularly with regard to level of detail in reporting, function versus program reporting, allocation of depreciation and indirect expenses, and prior-year data comparison (Q15). This chapter provides an explanation of the major concepts of the new statements and implementation recommendations that will result in enhanced financial statement/reporting comparability among school districts.

GOVERNMENTAL VERSUS BUSINESS-TYPE ACTIVITIES

The district-wide presentation distinguishes between "Governmental Activities" and "Business-type Activities." The distinction between these two categories is found in Statement 34, paragraph 15, which says, in part:

> Governmental activities generally are financed through taxes, intergovernmental revenues, and other non-exchange revenues. These activities are

9

usually reported in governmental funds and internal service funds. Business-type activities are financed in whole or in part by fees charged to external parties for goods or services. These activities are usually reported in enterprise funds.

The most common school district activity that may be classified as a business-type activity is the food service operation. Statement 34, paragraph 67, identifies the criteria that would necessitate the classification of such operations as business-type activities. In summary, if the activity is financed with debt that is secured solely by a pledge of the net revenues and fees and charges of the activity, or the laws and regulations require that costs be recovered by revenues of the activity, or the pricing policies of the activity are designed to fully recover all costs, then the activity should be classified as a business-type activity.

COMPONENT UNITS

The district-wide presentation requires that discretely presented component units (as opposed to blended component units) be presented in a column immediately to the right of the column that totals the district's governmental and business-type activities (Q17). A component unit is a legally separate entity for which the district is financially accountable. Examples could include a building project commission, a charter school, or an education foundation. As few districts actually have entities that meet the requirements for classification as a component unit, this guide will not address it in further detail.

STATEMENT OF NET ASSETS

The Statement of Net Assets is conceptually most closely related to a balance sheet in that it reports assets, liabilities, and the difference between them. It utilizes the accounting equation: assets minus liabilities equal net assets. The statement distinguishes between the district's governmental and business-type activities. If the district has a discretely presented component unit, there should be a separate column for reporting its assets, liabilities and net assets. The illustrative statement of net assets (Figure 2-1) does not present a column for a component unit.

ASSET PRESENTATION

The sample statement (Figure 2-1) is prepared in a classified format, which categorizes assets and liabilities as *current* and *non-current*. Use of

Figure 2-1   Illustrative District-Wide Statement of Net Assets.

ASBO, International School District
Statement of Net Assets
As of June 30, 2002

	Governmental Activities	Business-type Activities	Total
Assets			
Current assets:			
Cash and cash equivalents	$ 6,268,980	$ 328,243	$ 6,597,223
Investments	100,000,000	7,500,000	107,500,000
Taxes receivable (net)	12,182,730	-	12,182,730
Due from other governmental units	19,968,336	2,002,921	21,971,257
Other receivables	2,252,919	4,081	2,257,000
Interfund loans	615,597	(615,597)	-
Inventory and prepaid expenses	1,536,230	1,949,526	3,485,756
Other current assets	1,000	-	1,000
Total current assets	**142,825,792**	**11,169,174**	**153,994,966**
Non-current assets			
Restricted cash and cash equivalents	-	-	-
Capital assets	413,700,956	11,549,456	425,250,412
Less: Accumulated depreciation	(98,176,725)	(9,016,026)	(107,192,751)
Total non-current assets	**315,524,231**	**2,533,430**	**318,057,661**
Total assets	**458,350,023**	**13,702,604**	**472,052,627**
Liabilities			
Current liabilities:			
Accounts payable and other current liabilities	44,872,075	580,730	45,452,805
Deferred revenue	3,117,910	723,038	3,840,948
Current portion of long-term obligations	16,554,854	-	16,554,854
Total current liabilities	**64,544,839**	**1,303,768**	**65,848,607**
Non-current liabilities:			
Noncurrent portion of long-term obligations	102,242,026	-	102,242,026
Total non-current liabilities	**102,242,026**	**-**	**102,242,026**
Total liabilities	**166,786,865**	**1,303,768**	**168,090,633**
Net Assets			
Invested in capital assets, net of related debt	231,118,669	2,533,430	233,652,099
Restricted for:			-
Debt service	4,133,180	-	4,133,180
Capital Projects	-	-	-
Other activities	1,396,569	-	1,396,569
Unrestricted	54,914,740	9,865,406	64,780,146
Total net assets	**$ 291,563,158**	**$ 12,398,836**	**$ 303,961,994**

the classified format is not required. An alternate format is to present assets and liabilities in order of their relative *liquidity* or *maturity*, respectively. Assets most easily convertible to cash or consumed most quickly would be presented first. GASB prefers (but does not require) the liquidity presentation at the district-wide level, but requires the classified presentation for proprietary statements at the fund level (Q81).

CAPITAL ASSETS (Q25–29)

The most significant assets for most districts are their capital assets, such as land, buildings, and equipment. Some assets, such as land, that are inexhaustible and therefore are not depreciable, are reported in the statement of net assets at their historic cost or fair value at date of donation. Other assets, such as buildings and equipment, are exhaustible and therefore depreciable. The original or estimated historical cost of depreciable capital assets is also reported on the statement, net of accumulated depreciation. More detailed information about major classes of capital assets is presented in the notes to the financial statements.

LIABILITY PRESENTATION

Using the classified format, liabilities are distinguished between current and non-current. Under the liquidity format, liabilities are listed in order of how quickly they must be repaid, beginning with those that must be repaid earliest. Current liabilities include a variety of payables, such as amounts owed to employees and vendors. The most common long-term or non-current liabilities are amounts borrowed to construct buildings. Long-term debt payments are segregated into two parts: the portion that is due within one year and the remainder. In the classified format, the former is listed with the current liabilities and the latter with the non-current liabilities.

NET ASSETS

At the district-wide level, net assets will be reported in three categories: capital assets net of related debt, restricted assets, and unrestricted assets (Q85). The following descriptions are in layman's terms. The actual definitions can be found in Statement 34, paragraphs 33–36.

- "Net assets invested in capital assets, net of related debt" is defined as capital assets less the outstanding debts incurred by the district to buy or construct the capital assets and less accumulated depreciation (Q88–94). School district staff should analyze existing debt and ascertain whether it was issued in support of the purchase of capital asset(s). The district will need to establish a system to easily link the debt to related assets so that the "Invested in capital assets, net of related debt" line of the Statement of Net Assets may be easily determined.
- Net assets are considered restricted if their use is constrained to a particular purpose by statutes, rules, or other entities with authority over the district. The individual amounts restricted for various purposes are each identified by category. Restrictions may include amounts legally segregated for payment of debt, unspent amounts borrowed for capital projects, or the net assets of permanent funds.
- Unrestricted assets are the resources that do not fall into the first two categories. They can be used for any purpose, though they are not necessarily liquid. District designations of funds for purposes such as cash flow or other activities are reported here but are not identified separately (Q101–102).

School officials should be aware of the possibility of unrestricted deficits; however, deficits for the total net assets are unlikely. In some cases, a school district may maintain an unrestricted deficit because it has not accumulated resources to offset certain long-term liabilities, such as compensated absences, claims, or judgments.

STATEMENT OF ACTIVITIES

The Statement of Activities is conceptually most closely related to an income statement, in that it reports revenues, expenses and changes in net assets. It reports gross expenses, offsetting program revenues and net cost information at the function or program level for the current year. General revenues are reported separately from program revenues. (See Figure 2-2.) The significance of this statement is that, for the first time, there is a presentation of the district's net cost, financed by general revenues, of each major activity (Q103).

Figure 2-2 Illustrative District-Wide Statement of Activities.

ASBO, International School District
Statement of Activities
For the Year ended June 30, 2002

Functions/Programs	Expenses	Program Revenues			Net (Expenses) Revenue and Changes in Net Assets		
		Charges for Services	Operating Grants and Contributions	Capital Grants and Contributions	Government Activities	Business Type Activities	Total
Governmental activities:							
Instruction:							
Regular instruction	$ 187,819,890	$ 3,096,599	$ 22,105,041		$ (162,618,250)		$ (162,618,250)
Special education instruction	35,216,229		4,144,695		(31,071,534)		(31,071,534)
Vocational education	10,564,869	1,956,842	1,243,408		(7,364,619)		(7,364,619)
Other instruction	1,173,874	456,278	138,157		(579,439)		(579,439)
Total Instruction	234,774,862	5,509,719	27,631,301	-	(201,633,842)	-	(201,633,842)
Support services:							
Pupil services	37,311,861	2,986,172	4,203,974		(30,121,715)		(30,121,715)
Instructional staff services	6,715,981		756,698		(5,959,283)		(5,959,283)
General administration services	26,863,926		3,026,792		(23,837,134)		(23,837,134)
School administration services	9,365,149		1,055,183		(8,309,966)		(8,309,966)
Business services	5,164,191		491,856		(4,672,335)		(4,672,335)
Operations & maintenance of plant services	30,411,349		2,896,485		(27,514,864)		(27,514,864)
Pupil transportation services	8,606,985		819,759		(7,787,226)		(7,787,226)
Central services					-		-
Other support services	13,197,377		1,256,965		(11,940,412)		(11,940,412)
Community services	2,753,346		131,297		(2,622,049)		(2,622,049)
Interest on long-term debt	5,969,465				(5,969,465)		(5,969,465)
Depreciation - unallocated*	6,555,053				(6,555,053)		(6,555,053)
Total Support Services	152,914,683	2,986,172	14,639,009		(135,289,502)		(135,289,502)
Total governmental activities	387,689,545	8,495,891	42,270,310	-	(336,923,344)	-	(336,923,344)

Business-type activities:

	Expenses	Charges for Services	Operating Grants	Capital Grants	Governmental activities	Business-type activities	Total
Food services	20,596,032	4,750,350	15,849,235	$ 750,000		$ 753,553	753,553
Adult education	1,837,753	936,150	1,102,491			200,888	200,888
Total business-type activities	**22,433,785**	**5,686,500**	**16,951,726**	**750,000**		**954,441**	**954,441**
Total school district	**$ 410,123,330**	**$ 14,182,391**	**$ 59,222,036**	**$ 750,000**	**(336,923,344)**	**954,441**	**(335,968,903)**
General revenues:							
Taxes							
Property taxes, levied for general purposes					154,108,322		154,108,322
Property taxes, levied for debt services					16,860,557		16,860,557
Property taxes, levied for specific purposes (list each)					-		-
Other taxes							
Federal and State aid not restricted to specific purposes							
General					176,265,211		176,265,211
Other					-		-
Interest and investment earnings					7,397,103	312,271	7,709,374
Miscellaneous					-		-
Subtotal, general revenues					**354,631,193**	**312,271**	**354,943,464**
Excess (deficiency) of revenues over expenses before special items					**17,707,849**	**1,266,712**	**18,974,561**
Transfers							
Special items - gain on sale of unimproved land					1,367,341		1,367,341
Extraordinary items							
Total general revenues, transfers, special, and extraordinary items					**355,998,534**	**312,271**	**356,310,805**
Changes in net assets					**19,075,190**	**1,266,712**	**20,341,902**
Net assets - beginning					272,487,968	11,132,124	283,620,092
Net assets - ending					$ 291,563,158	$ 12,398,836	$ 303,961,994

*This amount excludes the appreciation that is included in the direct expenses of the various functions. See Note 2.

EXPENSES

The minimum requirement for presentation of expenses is by function, rather than by program. Most of the functional categories in Figure 2-2 are self-explanatory. However, there are a few functions that can be interpreted in a variety of ways depending upon individual state requirements. The following will be helpful in providing clarification for the following functions:

- Other instruction may include adult instruction that is not reported as part of community services, bilingual, gifted, summer school, extra and co-curricular programs, and instructional technology.
- Instructional staff services include improvement of instruction, learning media center, and student assessment and testing.
- General administration services include superintendent, board of education, and support services administration.
- Business services include fiscal services and data processing services.
- Central services include centrally provided services that are not charged back to individual functions, information services, and planning and research services.
- Depreciation (unallocated) includes the depreciation that has not been allocated to a specific expense function.

DEPRECIATION

The measurement focus and basis of accounting used in the statement of activities results in the need for depreciation of capital assets. As a result, items purchased and capitalized in the current year will not be reported as current expenses on the statement of activities. The depreciation for assets directly associated with a specific function or a small number of functions is required to be reported as a direct expense of that function(s). Consequently, the district will need to establish policies and procedures for identifying and classifying direct versus indirect assets at the time of purchase and whenever asset changes are made.

Depreciation of assets that serve essentially all functions may be allocated among the functions, included in a "general" expenses function or reported as a separate cost. *ASBO recommends reporting depreciation expense not directly related to specific functions on a separate line titled "Depreciation (unallocated)." Including depreciation expense in the general expenses function would inflate a cost to which many taxpayers already pay much attention.*

INDIRECT EXPENSE ALLOCATION (Q105–106)

GASB allows the district to include an indirect expense column to the right of the expenses column and allocate indirect expenses such as interest on long-term debt, depreciation (Q108) and general administration over the remaining functions of the district. *ASBO discourages this approach.* ASBO believes that some taxpayers would interpret this as an attempt to hide administrative costs among other functions. Further, there are a variety of allocation methods that districts could utilize, which would further complicate the process of achieving uniformity and comparability.

PROGRAM REVENUES

The columns to the right of gross expenses present the district's program revenues. These revenues are classified by the function for which they were earned (Q115–116). These are of two types:

- Charges for Services (Q117–118) are fees and other charges to the users or recipients of the services the district provides. This could include items such as: food service sales, rental fees for school buses or facilities, athletic participant or spectator fees, tuition, or library fines.
- Grants and Contributions (Q119–121) are funds the district receives that are restricted for a particular purpose. This could include items such as title programs, special education, transportation, and food and nutrition aid. The statement separates these grants into two categories:

- Operating—to finance the district's annual operating activities; and
- Capital—to fund the acquisition, construction, or renovation of capital assets.

Refer to Figure 2-3 for guidance on treatment various revenues.

NET COST OF SERVICES

The column titled "Net (Expenses) Revenue and Changes in Net Assets" is significant because it shows the net cost or revenue of each function of the school district. These dollar amounts are calculated by subtracting total program revenues from the expenses of each function. If the expenses of the district's functions surpass program revenues, negative numbers result in the statement, representing a net expense or net cost to the general public. These functions are generally dependent upon general-purpose revenues, including tax dollars. When program revenues exceed expenses, the resulting number is positive, representing a net revenue to

Figure 2-3　Illustrative Classification of Revenues by NCES Title.

NCES TITLE	PROGRAM REVENUES			GENERAL PURPOSE	SPECIAL/ EXTRAORDINARY ITEMS
	Charges for Services	Operating Grants and Contributions	Capital Grants and Contributions		
Property Taxes				Always	
Payments in Lieu of Taxes				Always	
Interfund Payments	Potentially	Potentially	Potentially	Potentially	
Payments for Services (tuition)	Generally			Potentially	
Food Service Sales	Always				
Non-Capital Sales	Generally			Potentially	
School Activity Income	Generally			Potentially	
Interest on Investments	Potentially			Generally	
Other Local Revenue	Potentially			Generally	
Interdistrict Transit of Aids	Potentially	Potentially	Potentially	Potentially	
Interdistrict Tuition Payment	Generally			Potentially	
Other Interdistrict Payments	Potentially	Potentially	Potentially	Potentially	
Intermediate Transit of Aids	Potentially	Potentially	Potentially	Potentially	
Intermediate Payment for Services	Generally			Potentially	
Other Intermediate Payments	Potentially	Potentially	Potentially	Potentially	
Categorical State Aid	Potentially	Potentially	Potentially	Potentially	
General State Aid				Always	
State Payments for Special Projects		Generally	Potentially		
State Tuition Payments	Generally			Potentially	
State Payments through Local Units	Potentially			Generally	
Federal Categorical Aid		Generally	Potentially		
Federal Impact Aid				Generally	
Federal Payments for Special Projects		Generally	Potentially		
Gain or Loss on Sale of Fixed Assets					Generally
Refund of Prior Year Disbursements				Generally	

the general public, sometimes available to offset other program costs. The "positive" and "negative" numbers should not be construed as value judgments. They are merely indicative of whether a particular function relies on general revenues for financing or is a net contributor of resources to the district.

GENERAL REVENUES

General revenues are presented immediately below the total net expense of the functions. General revenues represent the revenues available to the school district to finance the net cost of services not funded by program revenues.

The first major revenue source is "Property Taxes," which includes:

- Property taxes levied for general purposes such as property taxes for education, special education, and building operations;
- Property taxes levied for debt services such as property taxes for bonded debt that have resulted in a property tax levy schedule;
- Property taxes levied for specific purposes such as property taxes for tort immunity, transportation, fire prevention and safety, state retirement programs, and any other specifically segregated levy; and
- Other taxes such as taxes that are not derived from the property tax levy process (e.g., sales taxes).

The second major revenue source is federal and state aid not restricted to specific purposes. The presentation of these revenues is separated between General and Other. The remaining general revenue sources are interest and investment earnings (Q130) and miscellaneous. Refer to Figure 2-3 for guidance on treatment of various revenues.

TRANSFERS, SPECIAL ITEMS, EXTRAORDINARY ITEMS

Immediately below the general revenues, the district reports several other transactions and financial events that affect net assets. Transfers reflect financial transactions between governmental and business-type activities that are not based on receiving anything in return. Transfers between governmental and business-type activities are reported on the district-wide statements, and transfers within governmental and business-type activities are eliminated at the district-wide statement level.

Special items and/or extraordinary items are financial events that are unusual in nature and infrequent in occurrence (Q139–142). Definitions for these items can be found in Statement 34, paragraphs 55–56. They are shown separately from revenues and expenses specifically because they are not representative of the district's usual annual financial transactions.

NET ASSETS

The beginning and ending net assets are presented to reconcile the change in net assets.

Chapter Three

Fund Financial Statements

This chapter describes changes related to a district's fund financial statements. Chapter 6 explains the combining fund financial statements and a comprehensive annual financial report (CAFR). As described in Chapter 2, the district-wide financial statements provide an all-inclusive view. The fund financial statements provide a more detailed look at specific activities or groups of activities (Q157). The governmental fund financial statements are presented on a modified accrual basis, whereas governmental activities in the district-wide financial statements are presented on an accrual basis of accounting. The fund statements will be divided into governmental funds statements, proprietary funds statements and fiduciary funds statements.

The first significant change in the fund statements required by Statement 34 is a move from "fund-type" to "major fund" (Q175) presentation. Major fund presentation is required for governmental and enterprise funds. The school district will report each major fund in a separate column on the financial statements with all the non-major funds presented in a single column.

The district's most significant governmental and enterprise funds are considered major funds. The district's main operating fund (usually the general fund) is always reported as a major fund. A fund is classified as a major fund if (Q182–188, Appendix 4 and Exercise 5):

- Total assets, liabilities, revenues or expenditures/expenses of that individual governmental or enterprise fund are at least 10 percent of the corresponding total (assets, liabilities and so forth) of all funds of that category; *and*

- Total assets, liabilities, revenues or expenditures/expenses of the individual governmental fund or enterprise fund are at least 5 percent of the total for all governmental and enterprise funds combined.

The school district may also display any other governmental or enterprise fund as a major fund if it believes that the fund is important to the users of its financial statements. This criteria gives school districts the discretion to include the same funds from year to year for consistency, even if the criteria in (a) & (b) above are not met. Business officials should consider long-term reporting implications when exercising this option.

All funds that do not qualify as major are considered non-major funds (Q176). These funds are aggregated and presented in a single column. The major fund concept does not, however, apply to internal service or fiduciary funds.

Another change required by Statement 34 is that the concept of expendable and non-expendable trust funds is dropped and fiduciary funds are defined differently. Funds previously reported as non-expendable, whose resources are used to support school district operations, are now reported in a new governmental fund "permanent funds." Permanent funds account for resources legally restricted such that only the earnings they generate, and not the principal, may be used to finance operations (Q159). Funds previously reported as non-expendable, whose resources are NOT used to support school district operations, will continue to be reported in a fiduciary fund.

Funds previously reported as expendable fiduciary funds and whose resources are used to support district operations, are now reported in a special revenue fund. Previous expendable funds whose resources are NOT used to support district operations are reported in an agency fund.

GOVERNMENTAL FUNDS STATEMENTS

The governmental funds track the finances of a school district's basic services and, collectively, are virtually the same, after considering the different measurement focus and basis of accounting, as the governmental activities reported in the district-wide statements. They include the general, special revenue, debt service, capital projects, and the new permanent funds. Governmental fund statements represent a short-term financial view and tend to be focused on budgetary and/or regulatory compliance. Figure 3-1 presents an illustration of the Governmental Funds Balance Sheet and Figure 3-2 presents an illustration of the Governmental Funds Statement of Revenues, Expenditures, and Changes in Fund Balances. The district's major funds are presented in separate columns with all non-major funds presented in one column labeled *Other Governmental Funds* with all columns being totaled. If the school district wishes to present the

Figure 3-1   Illustrative Governmental Funds Balance Sheet.

ASBO, International School District
Balance Sheet
Governmental Funds
As of June 30, 2002

	General Fund	Debt Service Fund	Other Governmental Funds	Total Governmental Funds
ASSETS				
Cash and cash equivalents	$ 100,864,805	$ 3,294,850	$ 2,109,325	$ 106,268,980
Property taxes receivable	15,179,756	2,702,625	—	17,882,381
Less allowance for uncollectible taxes	(4,838,244)	(861,407)	—	(5,699,651)
Due from other governments	15,105,826	—	4,862,510	19,968,336
Accrued interest	504,757	—	—	504,757
Due from other funds	5,170,479	759,359	1,852,454	7,782,292
Other receivables	1,218,640	20,695	508,827	1,748,162
Inventories--supplies and materials	1,412,121	—	—	1,412,121
Other current assets	125,109	—	—	125,109
Total assets	**$ 134,743,249**	**$ 5,916,122**	**$ 9,333,116**	**$ 149,992,487**
LIABILITIES AND FUND BALANCES				
Liabilities:				
Accounts payable and accrued liabilities	$ 30,270,632	$ 8,740	$ 933,434	$ 31,212,806
Due to other funds	20,845,752	—	5,503,492	26,349,244
Due to other governments	10,093	—	—	10,093
Due to student groups	—	—	256,183	256,183
Deferred revenue	12,283,000	1,774,202	1,243,438	15,300,640
Amounts held for granting agencies	233,035	—	—	233,035
Total liabilities	**63,642,512**	**1,782,942**	**7,936,547**	**73,362,001**
Fund Balances:				
Reserved for:				
Inventories	1,412,121	—	—	1,412,121
Retirement of long-term debt	—	4,133,180	—	4,133,180
Encumbrances	4,744,173	—	—	4,744,173
Unreserved:				
Designated	21,347,665	—	—	21,347,665
Undesignated, reported in:				
General fund	43,596,778	—	—	43,596,778
Special revenue funds	—	—	1,396,569	1,396,569
Total fund balances	**71,100,737**	**4,133,180**	**1,396,569**	**76,630,486**
Total liabilities and fund balances	**$ 134,743,249**	**$ 5,916,122**	**$ 9,333,116**	**$ 149,992,487**

Figure 3-2 Illustrative Governmental Funds Statement of Revenues, Expenditures, and Changes in Fund Balances.

ASBO, International School District
Statement of Revenues, Expenditures and Changes in Fund Balances
Governmental Funds
For the Year Ended June 30, 2002

	General Fund	Debt Service Fund	Other Gov't Funds	Total Gov't Funds
Revenues:				
Property Taxes	153,862,367	16,589,425		170,451,792
Other Local Sources	8,404,240	194,926	124,789	8,723,955
Intermediate Sources	2,106,451		4,225,941	6,332,392
State Sources	188,019,530		6,135,833	194,155,363
Federal Sources	2,284,748		22,095,410	24,380,158
Other Sources	395,088		441,559	836,647
TOTAL REVENUES	**355,072,424**	**16,784,351**	**33,023,532**	**404,880,307**
Expenditures:				
Instruction:				
Regular Instruction	146,067,673		28,481	146,096,155
Special Instruction	33,937,539		25,907,721	59,845,259
Other Instruction	26,953,263			26,953,263
Total Instruction	**206,958,475**		**25,936,202**	**232,894,677**
Support Services				
Pupil Services	34,010,001		3,003,049	37,013,050
Instructional Staff Services	12,579,165		1,825,705	14,404,870
General Administration Services	9,290,149			9,290,149
Building Administration Services	18,906,114			18,906,114
Business Services	6,047,066			6,047,066
Operations & Maintenance	33,258,353			33,258,353
Pupil Transportation	16,310,144		1,308,415	17,618,559
Central Services	1,691,107			1,691,107
Community Services			1,040,189	1,040,189
Principal and Interest	1,538,918	15,894,705	504,668	17,938,291
Other Support Services	922,537		8,327	930,864
Total Support Services	**134,553,554**	**15,894,705**	**7,690,353**	**158,138,612**
TOTAL EXPENDITURES	**341,512,029**	**15,894,705**	**33,626,555**	**391,033,289**
Excess (deficiency) of revenues over expenditures	13,560,395	889,646	(603,023)	13,847,018
Other Financing Sources (Uses):				
Proceeds from Capital Leases			692,245	692,245
Special Items				
Proceeds from sale of unimproved lands	2,601,908			2,601,908
NET CHANGE IN FUND BALANCES	**16,162,303**	**889,646**	**89,222**	**17,141,171**
Fund Balance - Beginning	54,938,434	3,243,534	1,307,347	59,489,315
Fund Balance - Ending	71,100,737	4,133,180	1,396,569	76,630,486

non-major funds individually, it can do so by presenting these funds in combining financial statements (see Chapter 6).

Since the district-wide and fund financial statements use different bases of accounting, a reconciliation is required. The objective of this reconciliation is to describe the differences between the fund and district-wide statements. Both governmental fund statements must be reconciled to the governmental activities in the district-wide statements. These reconciliations may be presented directly on the fund statements or on an accompanying, separate statement following each fund statement. *ASBO recommends using a separate schedule for the reconciliation* (see Figures 3-3 and 3-4). This will allow for a more complete explanation of the reconciling items and may preclude the need for additional note disclosures.

The reconciliation for the balance sheet explains the differences between the total fund balance for the governmental funds statements and the total net assets reported on the government-wide statements. The reconciliation for the statement of revenues, expenditures, and changes in fund balances explains the differences between the net change in fund

Figure 3-3 Illustrative Reconciliation of Governmental Funds Balance Sheet to District-Wide Statement of Net Assets (Separate Statement Option).

ASBO, International School District
Reconciliation of the Governmental Funds Balance Sheet
with the Statement of Net Assets
June 30, 2002

Amounts reported for governmental activities in the statement of net assets are different because:

Total fund balance - governmental funds		**$76,630,486**
Capital assets used in governmental activities are not financial resources and therefore are not reported as assets in governmental funds.		
The cost of capital assets is	413,700,956	
Accumulated depreciation is	98,176,725	
		315,524,231
Property taxes receivable will be collected this year, but are not available soon enough to pay for the current period's expenditures, and therefore are deferred in the funds.		12,182,730
An internal service fund is used by the District's management to charge the costs of the unemployment compensation insurance program to the individual funds. The assets and liabilities of the internal service fund are included with governmental activities.		6,022,591
Long-term liabilities, including bonds payable, are not due and payable in the current period and therefore are not reported as liabilities in the funds. Long-term liabilities at year end consist of:		
Bonds payable	80,575,118	
Accrued interest on the bonds	759,880	
Capital leases payable	1,062,861	
Contracts payable	2,767,583	
Compensated absences (vacations)	1,125,503	
Special termination benefits payable	16,491,286	
In addition, in 1990, the district issued "capital appreciation" bonds (for example, the price of a bond was $640, but redeemable at maturity for $1,000). The accretion of interest on those bonds to date is	16,014,649	(118,796,880)
Total net assets--governmental activities		**$291,563,158**

Figure 3-4   Illustrative Reconciliation of Net Change in Fund Balances with Change in Net Assets (Separate Page Format).

ASBO, International School District
Reconciliation of the Governmental Funds Statement of Revenues, Expenditures, and Changes in Fund Balances
with the District-wide Statement of Activities
For the Year Ended June 30, 2002

Total net change in fund balances--governmental funds	$ 17,141,171

Amounts reported for governmental *activities* in the statement of activities are different because:

Capital outlays to purchase or build capital assets are reported in governmental funds as expenditures. However, for governmental activities those costs are shown in the statement of net assets and allocated over their estimated useful lives as annual depreciation expenses in the statement of activities. This is the amount by which depreciation exceeds capital outlays in the period.

	Depreciation expense $	13,108,809	
	Capital outlays	(930,864)	(12,177,945)

Some of the capital assets acquired this year were financed with capital leases. The amount financed by the leases is reported in the governmental funds as a source of financing. On the other hand, the capital leases are not revenues in the statement of activities, but rather constitute long-term liabilities in the statement of net assets.   (692,245)

Because some property taxes will not be collected for several months after the District's fiscal year ends, they are not considered as "available" revenues in the governmental funds, and are instead counted as deferred tax revenues. They are, however, recorded as revenues in the statement of activities.   517,087

In the statement of activities, only the *gain* on the sale of the unimproved land is reported, whereas in the governmental funds, the entire proceeds from the sale increase financial resources. Thus, the change in net assets differs from the change in fund balances by the *cost* of the land sold   (1,234,567)

In the statement of activities, certain operating expenses--compensated absences (vacations) and special termination benefits (early retirement)--are measured by the amounts *earned* during the year. In the governmental funds, however, expenditures for these items are measured by the amount of financial resources used (essentially, the amounts actually *paid*). This year, special termination benefits paid ($10,300,426) *exceeded* the amounts earned ($7,906,074) by $2,394,352. Vacation used ($261,132) was *less than* the amounts earned ($327,280) by $66,148.   2,328,204

Repayment of bond principal is an expenditure in the governmental funds, but it reduces long-term liabilities in the statement of net assets and does not affect the statement of activities.   13,526,946

Interest on long-term debt in the statement of activities differs from the amount reported in the governmental funds because interest is recorded as an expenditure in the funds when it is due, and thus requires the use of current financial resources. In the statement of activities, however, interest expense is recognized as the interest accrues, regardless of when it is due. The additional interest reported in the statement of activities is the net result of two factors. First, accrued interest on bonds, leases, and contracts payable *decreased* by $43,380. Second, $1,601,500 of additional accumulated interest was accreted on the district's "capital appreciation" bonds.   (1,558,120)

An internal service fund is used by the District's management to charge the costs of the unemployment compensation insurance program to the individual funds. The net revenue of the internal service fund is reported with governmental activities.   1,224,659

Change in net assets of governmental activities.	**$ 19,075,190**

balances for the combined governmental funds and changes in net assets for governmental activities. More disclosure may be provided in the notes to financial statements (see Figures 5-4 and 5-5 in chapter 5).

The statement of revenues, expenditures, and changes in fund balances contains the same major funds as the balance sheet. Revenues are classified by source, such as local revenue, property tax, and state aid. Expenditures are presented by function, the same as in the district-wide financial statements. The inclusion of debt service and capital outlay expenditures on the statement of revenues, expenditures, and changes in fund balances are the major differences from the district-wide expenses on the statement of activities. Statement 34 eliminated the General Fixed Assets and General Long-Term Debt Account Groups. Therefore, the assets and liabilities previously reported in the account groups are now reported only in the district-wide financial statements.

Figure 3-5   Illustrative Proprietary Funds Statement of Net Assets.

ASBO, International School District
Statement of Net Assets
Proprietary Funds
As of June 30, 2002

| | Business-Type Activities: Enterprise Funds | | | Governmental Activities: |
	Adult Education	Food Service	Total	Internal Service Fund
ASSETS				
Current Assets:				
Cash and cash equivalents	$ 1,857,211	$ 5,971,032	$ 7,828,243	-
Due from other governments	599,005	1,268,411	1,867,416	-
Due from other funds	-	-	-	$ 17,589,312
Other receivables	35,803	3,783	39,586	-
Inventories--supplies and materials	477,150	1,572,376	2,049,526	-
Total Current Assets	2,969,169	8,815,602	11,784,771	17,589,312.00
Noncurrent Assets:				
Furniture and equipment (net)	-	2,533,430	2,533,430	-
Total assets	2,969,169	11,349,032	14,318,201	17,589,312
LIABILITIES				
Current Liabilities				
Accounts payable and accrued liabilities	96,579	484,151	580,730	11,566,721
Due to other funds	173,058	442,539	615,597	—
Deferred revenue	202,003	521,035	723,038	—
Total Liabilities	471,640	1,447,725	1,919,365	11,566,721
NET ASSETS				
Invested in capital assets	—	2,533,430	2,533,430	—
Unrestricted	2,497,529	7,367,877	9,865,406	6,022,591
Total net assets	$ 2,497,529	$ 9,901,307	$ 12,398,836	$ 6,022,591

PROPRIETARY FUNDS STATEMENTS

Proprietary funds are activities that a school district operates similar to a business, in that they attempt to recover costs through charges to the user. The proprietary funds have not changed under Statement 34 and include the enterprise and internal service funds. However, the definitions of those fund types did change somewhat and should be reviewed by district staff.

Enterprise funds may be used to account for any activity or service that charges a fee to external users in order to cover the cost of operations, including costs of depreciation and debt service. An enterprise must be used to report activities that meet any of the following criteria:

- activities financed by debt that is secured solely by a pledge of the net revenues from fees and charges (i.e. revenue bonds), or
- laws or regulations require that the activity's costs of providing services, including capital costs (such as depreciation or debt service) be recovered with fees and charges, rather than with taxes or similar revenues, or
- the district's pricing policies establish fees and charges designed to recover its costs, including capital costs.

Internal service funds account for goods and services that are provided to other funds in return for a fee to cover the cost of operations, including costs of depreciation and debt service. Internal service funds may enter into transactions with other governments, providing that the reporting district is the predominant participant in the funds activities.

The proprietary funds statements include the statement of net assets; statement of revenues, expenses and changes in fund net assets; and a statement of cash flows prepared using the direct method. These statements use the accrual basis of accounting, similar to the district-wide statements. The statement of net assets is required to be prepared using the classified approach. Figure 3-5 illustrates the proprietary funds statement of net assets. The major enterprise funds are presented in individual columns and all non-major enterprise funds, if any, are aggregated and reported in a single column. The internal service funds are presented in a single column to the right of the total column for enterprise funds. Figure

3-6 illustrates the statement of revenues, expenses, and changes in fund net assets. Figure 3-7 illustrates the Statement of Cash Flows.

FIDUCIARY FUNDS STATEMENTS

The school district's fiduciary funds account for activity in which the school acts as a trustee or in an agency capacity for another party. These are resources that are not available to support district operations. There are four fiduciary fund types, which are pension (and other employee benefit) trust funds, investment trust funds, private purpose trust funds and agency funds (such as student activity funds). Therefore, fiduciary activities are not included in the district-wide statements because they are not available for district operations. The two statements required for fiduciary funds are the statement of fiduciary net assets and statement of changes

Figure 3-6   Illustrative Proprietary Funds Statement of Revenues, Expenditures, and Changes in Fund Net Assets.

ASBO, International School District
Statement of Revenues, Expenses, and Changes in Fund Net Assets
Proprietary Funds
For the Year Ended June 30, 2002

	Business-Type Activities: Enterprise Funds			Governmental Activities:
	Adult Education	Food Services	Total	Internal Service Fund
Operating revenues:				
Local and intermediate sources	$ 936,150	$ 4,750,350	$ 5,686,500	$ 23,864,586
Total operating revenues	936,150	4,750,350	5,686,500	23,864,586
Operating expenses:				
Payroll costs	888,793	10,494,786	11,383,579	—
Professional and contract services	—	343,439	343,439	—
Supplies and materials	67,228	8,773,317	8,840,545	—
Facility rental	826,746	—	826,746	—
Other operating costs	54,986	984,490	1,039,476	22,639,927
Total operating expenses	1,837,753	20,596,032	22,433,785	22,639,927
Operating income (loss)	(901,603)	(15,845,682)	(16,747,285)	1,224,659
Nonoperating revenues (expenses):				
Interest income	10,861	301,410	312,271	—
Grants	1,102,491	15,849,235	16,951,726	—
Total nonoperating revenues (expenses)	1,113,352	16,150,645	17,263,997	—
Income (loss) before capital contributions	211,749	304,963	516,712	1,224,659
Capital contributions	—	750,000	750,000	—
Change in net assets	211,749	1,054,963	1,266,712	1,224,659
Total net assets--Beginning	2,285,780	8,846,344	11,132,124	4,797,932
Total net assets--Ending	$ 2,497,529	$ 9,901,307	$ 12,398,836	$ 6,022,591

Figure 3-7 Illustrative Proprietary Funds Statement of Cash Flows.

ASBO, International School District
Statement of Cash Flows
Proprietary Funds
For the Year Ended June 30, 2002

	Business-Type Activities: Enterprise Funds			Governmental Activities:
	Adult Education	Food Services	Total	Internal Service Fund
CASH FLOWS FROM OPERATING ACTIVITIES				
Cash received from user charges	$ 1,052,578	$ 4,851,104	$ 5,903,682	—
Cash received from assessments made to other funds	—	—	— $	22,639,927
Cash payments to employees for services	(888,793)	(10,494,786)	(11,383,579)	—
Cash payments for insurance claims	—	—	—	(22,639,927)
Cash payments to suppliers for goods and services	(35,449)	(7,855,737)	(7,891,186)	—
Cash payments for facility use	(826,746)	—	(826,746)	—
Cash payments for other operating expenses	—	(2,593)	(2,593)	—
Net cash used for operating activities	(698,410)	(13,502,012)	(14,200,422)	—
CASH FLOWS FROM NONCAPITAL FINANCING ACTIVITIES				
Nonoperating grants received	897,983	15,564,368	16,462,351	—
CASH FLOWS FROM CAPITAL AND RELATED FINANCING ACTIVITIES				
Capital contributions	—	750,000	750,000	
Acquisition of capital assets	—	(1,522,918)	(1,522,918)	—
Net cash used for capital and related financing activities	—	(772,918)	(772,918)	
CASH FLOWS FROM INVESTING ACTIVITIES				
Interest on investments	10,861	301,410	312,271	—
Net increase in cash and cash equivalents	210,434	1,590,848	1,801,282	—
Cash and cash equivalents -- Beginning	1,646,777	4,380,184	6,026,961	—
Cash and cash equivalents -- Ending	$ 1,857,211	$ 5,971,032	$ 7,828,243	—
Reconciliation of operating income (loss) to net cash provided (used) by operating activities:				
Operating income (loss)	$ (901,603)	$ (15,845,682)	$ (16,747,285)	$ 1,224,659
Adjustments to reconcile operating income (loss) to net cash provided (used) by operating activities:				
Depreciation	—	981,897	981,897	—
Commodities used	—	1,684,867	1,684,867	—
Changes in assets and liabilities:				
receivables	97,996	100,754	198,750	(2,549,089)
inventories	113,226	210,239	323,465	—
accrued liabilities	(5,684)	(371,455)	(377,139)	1,324,430
deferred revenue	(2,345)	(262,632)	(264,977)	—
Net cash provided by operating activities	$ (698,410)	$ (13,502,012)	$ (14,200,422)	—

NONCASH NONCAPITAL FINANCING ACTIVITIES
During the year the District received $1,684,867 of food commodities from the US Department of Agriculture.

in fiduciary net assets. Figure 3-8 is an example of these statements, which are presented on the accrual basis of accounting. The fiduciary funds are presented by fund type rather than major funds. If the district has multiple funds, it may present combining statements for each of the fund types in its CAFR.

BUDGETARY COMPARISONS

School districts are required to prepare a budgetary comparison for their general fund and each major special revenue fund for which it legally

Figure 3-8   Illustrative Statement of Fiduciary Net Assets and Illustrative Statement of Changes in Fiduciary Net Assets.

ASBO, International School District
Statement of Fiduciary Net Assets
As of June 30, 2002

	Private-Purpose Trust	Agency Funds
ASSETS		
Cash and cash equivalents	$ 280,087	$ 101,959
Due from other governments	—	100,242
Accrued interest	23,853	—
Due from other funds	321,026	1,272,211
Total assets	**624,966**	**1,474,412**
LIABILITIES		
Accounts payable	1,450	14,911
Due to student groups	—	1,239,739
Due to other governments	—	219,762
Total liabilities	**1,450**	**1,474,412**
NET ASSETS		
Reserved for scholarships	585,221	
Unreserved	38,295	
Total Net Assets	**$ 623,516**	

ASBO, International School District
Statement of Changes in Fiduciary Net Assets
For the Year Ended June 30, 2002

	Private-Purpose Trusts
ADDITIONS	
Private donations	$ 24,480
District contribution	5,000
Interest	32,487
Total additions	**61,967**
DEDUCTIONS	
Scholarships awarded	36,644
Change in net assets	**25,323**
Net Assets--Beginning	598,193
Net Assets--Ending	$ 623,516

adopts an annual budget. This may be done as a statement included as part of the basic financial statements or as a schedule included as required supplementary information. At a minimum, there will be three columns in this schedule or statement: original budget; final budget and actual data presented on the budgetary basis. A fourth and fifth column may be added to report the variance between the original budget and the final budget and the final budget to the actual results (see Figure 3-9).

ASBO recommends presenting budgetary comparison information as a required supplementary information schedule. The district is required to provide a reconciliation if the budget is prepared on a basis other than GAAP (See Figure 3-10). For example, if the school district budgets are prepared on a cash basis, it must reconcile this schedule (or statement) to

Figure 3-9   Illustrative Budgetary Comparison Statement.

ASBO, International School District
Budgetary Comparison Schedule for the General Fund
For the Year Ended June 30, 2002

| | Budgeted Amounts | | Actual | Variances-- Positive (Negative) | |
	Original	Final	(GAAP Basis)	Original to Final	Final to Actual
Revenues:					
Property Taxes	$ 149,617,343	$ 151,571,192	$ 153,862,367	$ 1,953,849	$ 2,291,175
Other Local Sources	8,330,157	8,318,808	8,404,240	(11,349)	85,432
Intermediate Sources	1,773,000	1,885,500	2,106,451	112,500	220,951
State Sources	189,720,000	187,073,000	188,019,530	(2,647,000)	946,530
Federal Sources	2,137,500	2,250,000	2,284,748	112,500	34,748
Other Sources	364,500	364,500	395,088	-	30,588
Total revenues	351,942,500	351,463,000	355,072,424	(479,500)	3,609,424
Expenditures:					
Instruction:					
Regular Instruction	147,577,920	147,152,460	146,067,673	425,460	1,084,787
Special Instruction	34,288,430	34,189,580	33,937,539	98,850	252,041
Other Instruction	27,231,945	27,153,438	26,953,263	78,507	200,175
Total Instruction	209,098,295	208,495,478	206,958,475	602,817	1,537,003
Support Services:					
Pupil Services	34,413,082	34,694,864	34,010,001	(281,782)	684,863
Instructional Staff Services	12,185,382	12,411,520	12,579,165	(226,138)	(167,645)
General Administration Services	10,252,023	9,627,845	9,290,149	624,178	337,696
Building Administration Services	18,314,271	18,654,150	18,906,114	(339,879)	(251,964)
Business Services	6,442,400	6,442,400	6,047,066	-	395,334
Operations & Maintenance	35,078,360	35,432,695	33,258,353	(354,335)	2,174,342
Pupil Transportation	17,138,286	17,376,467	16,310,144	(238,181)	1,066,323
Central Services	1,725,361	1,721,536	1,691,107	3,825	30,429
Principal and Interest	1,531,812	1,531,812	1,538,918	-	(7,106)
Other Support Services	5,059,000	5,059,000	922,537	-	4,136,463
Total Support Services	142,139,977	142,952,289	134,553,554	(812,312.00)	8,398,735
Total expenditures	351,238,272	351,447,767	341,512,029	(209,495)	9,935,738
Excess (deficiency) of revenues over expenditures	704,228	15,233	13,560,395	(688,995)	13,545,162
SPECIAL ITEM					
Proceeds from sale of unimproved land	2,610,000	2,610,000	2,601,908	—	(8,092)
Net change in fund balances	3,314,228	2,625,233	16,162,303	(688,995)	13,537,070
Fund balance--Beginning	54,938,434	54,938,434	54,938,434	—	—
Fund balance--Ending	$ 58,252,662	$ 57,563,667	$ 71,100,737	$ (688,995)	$ 13,537,070

Figure 3-10   Illustrative Budgetary Comparison Reconciliation.

Note A—Explanation of Differences between Budgetary Inflows and Outflows and
GAAP Revenues and Expenditures for ASBO, International School District

	General Fund	Special Revenue Fund
Sources/inflows of resources		
Actual amounts (budgetary basis) "available for appropriation" from the budgetary comparison schedule	$92,370,775	$ 4,349,914
Differences—budget to GAAP:		
The fund balance at the beginning of the year is a budgetary resource but is not a current-year revenue for financial reporting purposes.	(2,742,799)	(1,618,441)
Transfers from other funds are inflows of budgetary resources but are not *revenues* for financial reporting purposes.	(129,323)	—
The proceeds from the sale of the park land are budgetary resources but are regarded as a *special item,* rather than revenue, for financial reporting purposes.	(3,476,488)	—
Total revenues as reported on the statement of revenues, expenditures, and changes in fund balances—governmental funds.	$86,022,165	$ 2,731,473
Uses/outflows of resources		
Actual amounts (budgetary basis) "total charges to appropriations" from the budgetary comparison schedule.	$90,938,522	$ 3,314,572
Differences—budget to GAAP:		
Encumbrances for supplies and equipment ordered but not received is reported in the year the order is placed for *budgetary* purposes, but in the year the supplies are received for *financial reporting* purposes.	(186,690)	(16,037)
Transfers to other funds are outflows of budgetary resources but are not *expenditures* for financial reporting purposes.	(2,034,659)	(344,146)
Total expenditures as reported on the statement of revenues, expenditures, and changes in fund balances—governmental funds.	$88,717,173	$ 2,954,389

the respective major governmental funds statement of revenues, expenditures, and changes in fund balances (Q245, 247–253). If the budgetary comparison is presented as RSI, any excess of expenditures over budgeted appropriations in the individual funds is required to be disclosed in the notes (Q254).

Chapter Four

Capital Assets and Depreciation

GASB Statement 34 requires that districts issue district-wide financial statements using the economic resources measurement focus and accrual basis of accounting. The cost of usage, called depreciation, is reported in the current fiscal period in district-wide statements. This is contrasted with the cost of acquisition that is reported in the fund statements.

Statement 34 requires certain disclosures related to capital assets. Specifically, details by major classes should:

- present governmental activities separately from business-type activities
- report capital assets that are depreciated separately from those that are not
- report historical cost separately from accumulated depreciation.

For each class the following information, if applicable, should be reported:

- Beginning and end-of-year balances
- Acquisitions
- Sales or other dispositions
- Current depreciation expense.

Additionally, the amount of depreciation expense for each of the functions reported in the statement of activities must be disclosed.

To implement Statement 34, business officials will need to prepare for retroactive recognition of depreciation of capital assets as well as establish systems for prospective reporting. In order to prepare for recognition of depreciation, the following tasks need to be performed:

1. Determine the level to which current capital asset records meet information needs necessary to comply with Statement 34.
2. Determine if there is a need to re-define capital assets (i.e., consider capitalization threshold), for purposes of compliance.
3. Determine the inventory of capital assets in service as of the effective date of Statement 34.
4. Review recent capital maintenance projects to ascertain those that should be capitalized.
5. Examine the historical or estimated historical cost for all capital assets. Valuations need to be objectively determined. Many districts will have asset values from the inception of the General Fixed Assets Account Group. Districts that choose to re-create records for Statement 34 compliance should consider the following information sources to assist with valuing the inventory.
   • Original purchase records
   • Bond documents
   • Professional appraisal or other services
6. Determine the year of purchase and the estimated useful life for existing capital assets.
7. Establish procedures to perpetuate the capital assets and depreciation system.
8. Determine the amount of accumulated depreciation at the implementation date and the amount of depreciation expense for the current period.
9. Determine salvage value, if any.

A capital asset is reported and, with certain exceptions discussed later in this chapter, depreciated in district-wide statements. In the district-wide statements, assets that are not capitalized are expensed in the year of acquisition. The following information reviews and supplements information required to comply with pronouncements of GASB and FASB in regard to accounting for capital assets.

ASSET INVENTORY (Q67)

School districts should develop strategies to ensure that they have an accurate and up-to-date record of capital assets. School districts should have such an inventory beginning in 1980 when NCGA Statement #1 created the General Fixed Assets Account Group. School districts without an inventory will need to have one prepared as of the start of the year in which Statement 34 is implemented. The district will need to devise a method to determine historical costs or estimated historical cost of capital assets on hand. The district will further need to establish a system to perpetuate the capital asset inventory. Future asset acquisitions will be valued at the acquisition cost for purchased items. Items that are donated will be valued at the fair market value on the date of donation and depreciated over its remaining estimated useful life.

School districts need to have an inventory of all assets to be capitalized. Each inventory record will need to include: description, year of acquisition, method of acquisition (purchase or donation), funding source, cost or estimated cost, estimated useful life and salvage value. The inventory will also need to identify the function that uses the asset. The inventory need only include those assets that meet the definition of a capital asset, as determined by the school district. (See Q233 about reporting assets by "class" of assets.)

Capital assets include sites (land), site improvements, buildings, building improvements, furniture, fixtures and equipment, vehicles, and other items that meet criteria established by the school district. Districts will need to consider several criteria when deciding what assets to capitalize.

Land (Q27, 34, 276)

Land is not a depreciable asset. It is recorded at historical cost and remains at that cost until disposal. If there is a gain or loss on the sale or disposal of land, it is reported as a special item in the statement of activities.

Site Improvements (Q25)

Site improvements include items such as excavation, non-infrastructure utility installation, driveways, sidewalks, parking lots, flagpoles, retaining walls, fencing, outdoor lighting, and other non-building improvements intended to make the land ready for its intended purpose. Depreciation of site improvements is necessary if the improvement is exhaustible. Expenditures for improvements that do not require maintenance or replacement, expenditures to bring land into condition to commence erection of structures, expenditures for improvements not identified with structures, and expenditures for land improvements that do not deteriorate with use or passage of time are additions to the cost of land and are generally not exhaustible and therefore not depreciable. Other improvements that are part of a site, such as parking lots, landscaping and fencing, are usually exhaustible and are therefore depreciable.

Buildings and Construction in Progress (Q30–32, 34, 36–37)

Buildings should be recorded at either their acquisition cost or construction cost. The cost of new construction should be carefully evaluated. Usually projects consist of major components such as land, land improvements, building construction (including professional fees and permits), furniture, fixtures and equipment. The value of each component needs to be determined because different useful lives and salvage values may apply. Further, interest paid during the construction of assets subsequent to Statement 34 is added to the construction cost.

Construction in progress should not be depreciated. It should be reported with land and other non-depreciating assets at the district-wide level. Unspent debt proceeds from capital assets-related debt should be reported in the net assets section of the statement of net assets as "restricted for capital projects" net of its related debt, which will result in a net asset of zero dollars, unless a payment has already been made toward the related debt (Q89–90).

Building Improvements

Building improvements that extend the useful life should be capitalized. School districts should therefore review major maintenance projects for the last several years to determine those that should become part of the assets.

Examples of building improvements include roofing projects, major energy conservation projects, or remodeling and replacing major building infrastructure. A district will need to determine the practicality of identification of these projects, and prepare an inventory. The inventory will need to include a project description, the year completed, funding source and dollar amount. Only those projects that meet the capitalization threshold need to be included.

Personal Property (Q26)

Assets such as vehicles, furniture and equipment that meet threshold levels set by the district should be identified and inventoried. Some assets, individually, may fall below the capitalization threshold, but may be purchased in large quantities by the district. Examples include library books, textbooks, and computers. Districts may choose to capitalize these assets as groups. *ASBO recommends this be done if the assets are purchased with debt proceeds so that there is an asset to offset the debt on the statement of net assets.*

Infrastructure

Generally, school districts will have few, if any, infrastructure assets. Infrastructure assets are long-lived capital assets that normally can be preserved for a significantly greater number of years than most capital assets and that are normally stationary in nature. Examples include roads, bridges, tunnels, drainage systems, water systems, and dams. Infrastructure assets do not include buildings, drives, and parking lots or any of the above examples that are incidental to a school's property or access to the property. This guide does not address reporting requirements for infrastructure assets. If a school district determines it has these assets, the district should refer to publications of the GASB for guidance.

Criteria for Determination of Capital Assets

Estimated useful life. The first criterion is useful life. An asset must have an estimated useful life greater than one reporting period to be considered for capitalization and depreciation. Assets that are consumed, used-up, habitually lost or worn-out in one year or less should not be capitalized.

Estimated useful life means the estimated number of months or years that an asset will be able to be used for the purpose for which it was purchased. In determining useful life, districts should consider the asset's present condition, use of the asset, construction type, maintenance policy, and how long it is expected to meet service demands. Useful lives should be based on the districts own experience and plans for the assets. Although the standard useful life table presented here provides guidance, property management practices, asset usage, and other variables such as weather, may require adjustment to the recommended lives. Schedules of depreciable lives established by federal or state tax regulations are not necessarily representative of useful lives.

School districts may choose to depreciate assets individually or by grouping assets. If the district elects to group assets, the estimated life of the group may be based on the weighted average or simple average of the useful life of individual items, or on assessment of the life of the group as a whole. (See Appendix 4, Exercise #2 of the GASB Implementation Guide)

It may be necessary to make adjustments to the estimated useful life of to specific assets or groups of assets, depending on the overall condition. As with the determination of value, useful life can be determined by district staff or a professional appraiser (Q47–51).

Figure 4-1 represents guidelines developed by ASBO to assist school districts with estimating useful lives of capital assets. The table is based on data developed by a national property valuation firm. The ASBO committee adjusted portions of the data and added several new classifications. The table should not be implemented without careful consideration of local factors that may impact an asset's useful life. Further, it is likely that school districts will have assets that are not included in the figure. For example, some districts may own cattle that they wish to capitalize. Each district is responsible for developing a rational system for identifying which assets to capitalize and their associated lives.

Asset cost. The second criterion for determining depreciable capital assets is cost (Q29). School districts do not need to capitalize every asset with a useful life greater than one year. To do so is an unnecessary burden and will not materially effect financial results. School districts may wish

Figure 4-1   ASBO Guidelines for Estimating Lives of Capital Assets.

ASSET CLASS	EXAMPLES	Est. Useful Life
Land		N/A
Site Improvements	Paving, flagpoles, retaining walls, sidewalks, fencing, outdoor lighting	20
School Buildings		50 to 100
Portable Classrooms		25
HVAC Systems	Heating, ventilation, and air conditioning systems	20
Roofing		20
Interior Construction		25
Carpet Replacement		7
Electrical / Plumbing		30
Sprinkler / Fire System	Fire suppression systems	25
Outdoor Equipment	Playground, radio towers, fuel tanks, pumps	20
Machinery & Tools	Shop & maintenance equipment, tools	15
Kitchen Equipment	Appliances	15
Custodial Equipment	Floor scrubbers, vacuums, other	15
Science & Engineering	Lab equipment, scientific apparatus	10
Furniture & Accessories	Classroom and office furniture	20
Business Machines	Fax, duplicating & printing equipment	10
Copiers		5
Communications Equip.	Mobile, portable radios, non-computerized	10
Computer Hardware	PC's, printers, network hardware	5
Computer Software	Instructional, other short-term	5-10
Computer Software	Administrative or long-term	10-20
Audio Visual Equip.	Projectors, cameras (still & digital)	10
Athletic Equipment	Gymnastics, football, weight machines, wrestling mats	10
Musical Instruments	Pianos, string, brass, percussion	10
Library Books	Collections	5-7
Licensed Vehicles	Buses, other on-road vehicles	8 to 20
Contractors Equipment	Major off-road vehicles, front-end loaders, large tractors, mobile air compressor	10
Grounds Equipment	Mowers, tractors, attachments	15

to establish a dollar threshold as a basis for considering an asset for capitalization. Care should be taken when determining the threshold. A threshold that is too low may result in a burdensome record keeping system. A threshold that is too high could cause material misstatement of the district's financial condition. Consideration should be given to the diminishing returns of progressively lower capitalization levels. The above discussion is primarily intended to address the accounting threshold. School districts may chose to establish a different threshold for other purposes, such as control or insurance.

Figures 4-2 through 4-4 show the number of assets and total asset value for various capitalization thresholds for large, medium and small school districts. The exhibits illustrate that the number of assets is reduced significantly as the threshold increases. However, the total dollar value of

Figure 4-2   Capitalization Thresholds for Large School Districts.

Threshold	Number of Assets	Capitalized Value (In thousands)	Change
$1	50,000+	$90,000	
$300	9,529	$87,329	3.0%
$500	7,196	$86,376	4.0%
$1,000	4,384	$84,444	6.2%
$2,000	2,235	$81,022	10.0%
$5,000	478	$76,075	15.5%

Figure 4-3   Capitalization Thresholds for Medium School Districts.

Threshold	Number of Assets	Capitalized Value (In thousands)	Change
$1	12,000+	$27,700	
$300	2,476	$26,786	3.3%
$500	2,065	$26,619	3.9%
$1,000	1,304	$26,059	6.1%
$2,000	360	$24,736	10.7%
$5,000	167	$24,175	12.7%

Figure 4-4   Capitalization Thresholds for Small School Districts.

Threshold	Number of Assets	Capitalized Value (In thousands)	Change
$1	n/a	$2,929	
$300	896	$2,830	3.4%
$500	608	$2,723	7.0%
$1,000	324	$2,521	13.9%
$2,000	98	$2,189	25.3%
$5,000	36	$2,007	31.5%

*Data from the exhibits above was provided by a national appraisal firm.

capitalized assets is reduced only slightly. With a capitalization threshold of $5,000, large and medium sized school districts would easily account for 80% of their assets. Small school districts will need a capitalization threshold of $1,000 to achieve the standard.

The Government Finance Officers Association (GFOA) suggests a capitalization threshold of an amount that ensures that at least 80% of the value of assets are reported, but the threshold should not be greater than $5,000. The federal government also uses a capitalization threshold of $5,000 for federal grant management purposes. The capitalization threshold chosen by the district will depend on a number of factors. School districts need to consider state regulations and guidelines, auditor interpretations and the amount of associated debt, if any. *ASBO recommends that school districts establish a capitalization threshold that insures that at least 80% of the value of assets is reported, however the threshold should not be greater than $5,000.*

Improvements that extend the estimated useful life of sites or buildings should be capitalized. A higher capitalization threshold, such as $10,000 to $50,000, may be appropriate for these expenditures.

Prospective application of the requirement to capitalize and depreciate certain assets can be achieved by making certain that purchasing procedures provide for the collection of all necessary data. Subsequently, information on the acquisition cost of an asset should be readily available. Acquisition cost includes shipping, setup, and installation. Other costs, such as plumbing or electrical, incurred to place a new asset in service, should be included in the asset's acquisition cost. Further, interest cost is to be capitalized as a component of historical cost (Q30–31).

Districts need to develop a means to objectively determine historical or estimated historical costs for assets owned by the district as of the effective date of Statement 34, if this had not been previously accomplished. Purchase records are generally the most accurate source of information. The cost to peruse and evaluate purchase records, except for the most recent years, is likely to be greater than the benefit achieved by having historical cost data. As an alternative,

- Districts should consider the services of a professional property appraisal firm. Property appraisal firms are able to perform the asset inventory, to provide estimated historical cost information, and to give an objective estimate of the asset's useful life that will generally be acceptable to auditors. The American Institute of Certified Public Accountants' Industry Audit Guide, *Audits of State and Local Governmental Units,* states "a government may use outside professional assistance to appraise property."
- Often long-term debt is used to finance the purchase of capital assets. The total amount of original debt issuance may be an acceptable starting point to help to determine historical cost of some assets (Q274).

Associated debt. The third criterion is associated debt (Q274). School districts should carefully consider the merits of capitalizing assets purchased with debt proceeds. Doing so may minimize the potential of negative net assets being reported in the statement of net assets.

DEPRECIATION

In accounting terms, depreciation is the process of allocating the cost of tangible property over a period of time, rather than deducting the cost as an expense in the year of acquisition. Generally, at the end of an asset's life, the sum of the amounts charged for depreciation in each accounting period (accumulated depreciation) will equal original cost less salvage value. Good accounting and financial management practices require that a district take both the cost expiration and the declining value of an asset into account. The cost expiration of a district's assets must be recognized if the cost of providing services is to be realistically reported. Also, the decline in the value of those assets must be considered if the district's net assets are to be stated correctly. To be depreciated, a capital asset must:

- Be in use in the district,
- Have an estimated useful life greater than 1 year,
- Be subject to wear, decay, or expiration, and
- Be fully installed and ready for use.

To calculate depreciation on a capital asset, five factors must be known:

- The date the asset was placed in service,
- The asset's cost or acquisition value,
- The asset's salvage value,
- The asset's estimated useful life, and
- The depreciation method.

For general capital assets, depreciation is reported only on district-wide financial statements. Depreciation expense is reported on the Statement of Activities. Statement 34 requires that depreciation for assets specifically identified with specific functions are to be included in the direct expenses of those functions. Capital assets that serve essentially all functions are reported on a separate line or reported as part of the general administration (or its counterpart) function. If depreciation is reported as a separate line item, the face of the statement must clearly indicate that this line item excludes depreciation expense charged to functions.

ASBO recommends allocating the depreciation of a building that serves a few functions. ASBO recommends that the allocation be based on square footage for the time used.

Capital assets and the associated accumulated depreciation are reported in the statement of net assets. Accumulated depreciation may be reported separately, or capital assets may be presented net of accumulated depreciation on the statement.

The method used to calculate an asset's depreciation is important because depreciation reduces net assets. Accelerated depreciation methods reduce net assets more quickly than straight-line depreciation methods. In practical terms, depreciation suggests a gradual decline in an asset's value because of use. Statement 34 requires that school districts expense a specified amount each year to represent the cost of the actual use of a capital asset. This amount is treated as an expense even though the district may not have purchased the asset in the current period.

Averaging Conventions

To avoid the complications of depreciating each asset from the specific date on which it was placed in service, Generally Accepted Accounting Principles (GAAP) support guidelines that assume various assets are placed in service or disposed of at designated dates throughout the year. These guidelines are called averaging conventions.

There are five averaging conventions, as described below, in common use. *ASBO recommends school districts use the full-month convention.* The other conventions are described so business officials have an understanding of the available options.

Under a *full-month convention*, property placed in service at any time during a given month is treated as if it had been placed in service on the first of that month. This allows depreciation to be taken for the entire month in which the asset is placed in service. If the property is disposed of before the end of the recovery period, no depreciation is allowed for the month in which the property is disposed of.

Under the *half-year convention*, an asset is treated as though it were placed in service or disposed of on the 1st day of the 7th month of the fiscal year. One-half of a full year's depreciation is allowed for the asset in its first year placed in service, regardless of when it was actually placed in service during that year.

Under the *modified half-year convention*, assets placed in service during the first half of the year are considered to have been placed in service on the first day of the year. Therefore, they receive a full year's depreciation in the acquisition year. Assets placed in service during the second half of the year are considered to have been placed in service on the first day of the following year. Therefore, they receive no depreciation in the acquisition year but receive a full year's depreciation in the subsequent year.

Applying the modified half-year convention in the disposal year is slightly more complicated because the disposal-year allowance depends on the acquisition year allowance. Figure 4-5 summarizes the relationships. ASBO urges caution with adopting this averaging convention for large capital assets due to the possibility that misstatement of asset values and depreciation could occur.

Under the *mid-month convention*, property is treated as though it were placed in service or disposed of in the middle of the month. A half-month's depreciation is allowed both in the month of acquisition and in the month of disposition. Generally this means that if the asset is placed in service after the 15th of the month, no depreciation is taken for that month. If the asset is placed in service on or before the 15th of the month, a full month's depreciation is allowed. Similarly, if the asset is disposed

Figure 4-5   Averaging Convention Relationships.

If Asset Was Placed in Service in the:	And Disposed of in the:	Amount of Depreciation Allowed in the Disposal Year:
1st half of year	1st half of year	No depreciation
1st half of year	2nd half of year	50% of full year depreciation
2nd half of year	1st half of year*	50% of full year depreciation
2nd half of year	2nd half of year**	Full year of depreciation

*Refers to a year subsequent to the year of acquisition.
**To earn the full year of depreciation, the disposal must have been in a year after the acquisition year.

of on or before the 15th of the month, no depreciation is taken for that month. If the asset is disposed of after the 15th of the month, a full month's depreciation is allowed.

The *mid-quarter convention* treats property as though it were placed in service in the middle of the quarter in which it was purchased.

Depreciable Cost

An asset's depreciable cost is the amount of the asset's value for which a district will claim depreciation. A percentage of this basis is deducted each year. The depreciable cost is often (but not always) the cost or acquisition value of the asset. Under some depreciation methods, salvage value is considered in the determination of the depreciable cost.

One measure of an asset's depreciable cost is its purchase price. If something other than cash is used to pay for the asset, then the fair market value of the non-cash payment or consideration determines the depreciable cost. A non-cash consideration often takes the form of an account payable or an obligation to pay. When the value of the consideration paid can't be determined, the fair market value of the asset determines its depreciable cost.

With few exceptions, an asset's depreciable cost should also include necessary costs incurred to place the asset in service. These costs will be capitalized, not expensed. Costs that should be capitalized include the invoice price plus incidental costs (insurance during transit, freight, capitalized interest as described earlier, duties, title search, registration fees, and installation costs). Exceptions to this rule include interest expenses associated with deferred payments and real estate taxes paid, if any, in the acquisition of property.

The salvage value of an asset is the value it is expected to have when it is no longer useful. In other words, the salvage value is the amount for which the asset could be sold for at the end of its useful life.

Straight-line, sum-of-the-years'-digits, and some other depreciation methods require that the salvage value be subtracted from an asset's acquired value to determine its depreciable basis. Other methods, such as declining-balance, do not subtract the salvage value to determine the basis. However, the asset will not be depreciated below its salvage value.

Depreciation Methods

There are many different methods used to calculate depreciation. Some methods allow more depreciation in early years than in later years. Some apply the same percentage each year while the basis declines. Others apply different percentages each year while the basis remains the same.

The same depreciation method is not required for all capital assets. Further, depreciation may be calculated for a class of assets, a group of assets or individual assets. Once a method for a particular asset is chosen, however, it must generally be used for the life of the asset. *ASBO recommends that school districts use the straight-line depreciation method.* However, any established method of depreciation is acceptable by Statement 34. The straight-line depreciation method is described in greater detail below. Appendix 2 provides explanations and examples of alternate depreciation methods.

The straight-line method is the simplest and most commonly used for calculating depreciation. It can be used for any depreciable property. Under the straight-line depreciation method, the basis of the asset is written off evenly over the useful life of the asset. The same amount of depreciation is taken each year. In general, the amount of annual depreciation is determined by dividing an asset's depreciable cost by its estimated life.

The total amount depreciated can never exceed the asset's historic cost less salvage value. At the end of the asset's estimated life, the salvage value will remain.

For example, a $12,000 copier is placed in service on March 16, 2000. It has an estimated life of 5 years and a salvage value of $2,000. The depreciation calculation for the straight-line method would be:

Original cost	$12,000
Salvage value	$ 2,000
Adjusted basis	$10,000
Estimated Life	5 years
Depreciation per year	$ 2,000

A full-year's depreciation would be $2,000. Under a full-month convention, property placed in service at any time during a given month is treated as if it had been placed in service on the first of that month. This permits depreciation for the entire month in which the asset is placed in service. If the property is disposed of before the end of the recovery period, no depreciation is allowed for the disposal month. The full-month convention allows depreciation for the month of March. The depreciation for the fiscal year ended June 30, 2000, would be 3/12ths of the annual depreciation or $500.00.

Under the mid-month convention, the copier is considered to be placed in service in April, so the depreciation for the fiscal year ended June 30, 2000, would be 2/12ths of the annual depreciation or $333.33.

Chapter Five

Notes to the Financial Statements

The notes to financial statements provide additional information to the reader that has not been presented on the face of the financial statements (for reasons of practicality) but is essential for the financial statements to be fairly presented. This is why the phrase "The notes to the financial statements are an integral part of this statement" is included on the bottom of each basic financial statement. A district must determine which notes are necessary to ensure that the financial statements are fairly presented. Refer to the list in Figure 5-1 for examples of notes that may be applicable.

This chapter will highlight the major changes required by Statement 34. These changes effect the note disclosures for the summary of significant accounting policies, notes on capital assets and long-term liabilities and adds detailed information to reconcile the fund financial statements to the district-wide statements, if necessary.

SUMMARY OF SIGNIFICANT ACCOUNTING POLICIES

The changes in the summary of significant accounting policies are as follows:

- Description of district-wide statements, noting exclusion of fiduciary activity (Q230).
- Measurement focus and basis of accounting used in the district-wide and funds financial statements.

Figure 5-1 Selected Current Note Disclosures.

These two lists of note disclosures have been adapted from the GASB's *Codification of Governmental Accounting and Financial Reporting Standards.*

Notes that are essential if the information in the financial statements is to be presented fairly include:

a. Summary of significant accounting policies
b. Cash deposits with financial institutions
c. Investments
d. Significant **contingent liabilities** (such as pending lawsuits or unfilled purchase orders)
e. Significant effects of events subsequent to the end of the year
f. Annual pension cost and net pension obligations
g. Material violations of finance-related legal and contractual provisions
h. Future debt service requirements for currently outstanding debt
i. Commitments under operating leases

j. Construction and other significant commitments
k. Required disclosures about capital assets
l. Required disclosures about long-term liabilities
m. Deficit fund balance or net assets of individual funds
n. Receivables and payables between funds
o. Significant transactions between discretely presented component units and with the primary government
p. Disclosures about donor-restricted endowments
q. Interfund transfers

Additional note disclosures should be made if applicable to the government, including:

a. Risk management activities
b. Property taxes
c. Condensed financial statements for major discretely presented component units
d. Budget basis of accounting and budget-GAAP reporting differences not otherwise reconciled in the financial statements (Required only if schedule is presented as a basic statement.)
e. Short-term debt instruments and liquidity
f. Transactions with related parties
g. The nature of the district's accountability for related organizations
h. Capital leases
i. Joint ventures and jointly governed organizations
j. Debt refunding (similar to refinancing a mortgage)
k. Methods of estimating fixed asset costs
l. Designations of fund balance amounts
m. **Interfund eliminations** in fund financial statements not apparent from headings

n. Pension plans
o. Bond, tax, or revenue anticipation notes excluded from fund or current liabilities (proprietary funds)
p. Nature and amount of inconsistencies in financial statements caused by transactions between component units having different fiscal year-ends or changes in component unit fiscal year-ends
q. Reverse repurchase and dollar reverse repurchase agreements
r. Securities lending transactions
s. Demand bonds
t. Post-employment benefits other than pension benefits (like health insurance)
u. **On-behalf payments** for fringe benefits and salaries
v. Sponsoring government disclosures about external investment pools reported as investment trust funds
w. The amount of interest expense included in direct expenses (Q114)
x. Nonexchange transactions

- Policy for eliminating internal activity in the district-wide statement of activities.
- Policy for applying FASB pronouncements to business-type activities and to enterprise funds.
- Policy for capitalizing assets and for estimating the useful lives of those assets.
- Description of types of transactions included in program revenues
- Policy for defining operating and non-operating revenues of proprietary funds.
- Policy regarding application of restricted resources when an expense is incurred for purposes for which both restricted or unrestricted net assets are available.
- Policy for allocating indirect expenses to functions in the district-wide statement of activities.

Remember, the notes explain the accounting methods and assumptions used by the school district when reporting financial transactions in its financial statements.

CAPITAL ASSETS (Q232 AND 233)

One of the most significant changes a school district will encounter in implementing Statement 34 is depreciating its capital assets at the district-wide reporting level, which was discussed in Chapter 4. School districts are required to spread the cost of the assets over the estimated useful lives of the assets. Therefore, more detailed information about the district's capital assets is required to be explained in the notes to financial statements (see Figure 5-2). Prior financial statements presented general fixed assets at cost or estimated historical cost until the assets were sold or destroyed. Under the new model, assets will be depreciated over their useful lives, and when an asset is sold, destroyed, or otherwise becomes unusable to the district, it will be removed from the capital asset and accumulated depreciation accounts. The amounts of depreciation expense charged to each of the functions in the statement of activities should be disclosed.

Figure 5-2   Illustrative Capital Assets Note Disclosure.

Note 2—Disclosure of Information about Capital Assets

Capital asset balances and activity for the year ended June 30, 2002 were as follows (in thousands):

	Beginning Balance	Additions	Retirements/ Reclassifications	Ending Balance
Governmental activities:				
Land	$ 22,059	—	$ (1,235)	$ 20,824
Construction in progress	11,436	$ 40	—	11,448
Buildings	250,090	674	(10)	250,754
Furniture and equipment	135,275	217	(4,817)	130,675
Totals at historical cost	418,860	931	(6,062)	413,701
Less accumulated depreciation for:				
Buildings	61,547	11,345	(10)	72,882
Furniture and equipment	28,330	1,764	(4,799)	25,295
Total accumulated depreciation	89,877	13,109 *	(4,809)	98,177
Governmental activities capital assets, net	$ 328,983	$(12,178)	$ (1,253)	$315,524
Business-type activities:				
Furniture	$ 3,057	$ 344	—	$ 3,401
Equipment	6,881	1,267	—	8,148
Totals at historical cost	9,938	1,611	—	11,549
Less accumulated depreciation for:				
Furniture	1,649	364	—	2,013
Equipment	6,385	618	—	7,003
Total accumulated depreciation	8,034	982	—	9,016
Business-type activities capital assets, net	$ 1,904	$ 629	—	$ 2,533

* Depreciation expense was charged to governmental functions as follows:

Depreciation not allocated to specific functions	$ 6,555
Instruction	4,106
Pupil Services	587
General Administration Services	653
School Administration Services	164
Operations & Maintenance of Plant Services	996
Transportation	48
Total	$ 13,109

LONG-TERM LIABILITIES

A note in the financial statements should explain in detail a school district's long-term debt (see Figure 5-3 and Q234). Governmental and business-type activities are shown separately with major categories of long-term liabilities listed (e.g. general bonded debt, lease purchase, notes payable, compensated absences, termination pay, claims and judgments). The district should present the beginning balance, additions, reductions, ending balance and amount due within one year in columnar format. The amount due within one year will tie to the district-wide statement of net assets as the "current portion of long-term obligations." The note should

Figure 5-3   Illustrative Long-Term Debt Note Disclosure.

Note 3—Disclosure of Information about Long-term Liabilities

Long-term liability balances and activity for the year ended June 30, 2002 were as follows (in thousands):

Governmental Activities	Beginning Balance	Additions	Reductions	Ending Balance *	Amounts Due within One Year
General Obligation Debt					
Bonds & Notes Payable	$ 108,221	—	$ 11,710	$ 96,511	$ 12,875
Lease-purchase obligations	2,029	$ 692	1,356	1,365	1,063
Contractual obligations	3,765	—	461	3,304	461
Total bonds and notes payable	114,015	692	13,527	101,180	14,399
Other liabilities:					
Accumulated termination pay	18,885	7,906	10,300	16,491	1,961
Claims and judgments	10,243	6,959	5,635	11,567	5,700
Compensated absences	1,060	327	261	1,126	195
Total other liabilities	30,188	15,192	16,196	29,184	7,856
Total long-term liabilities	$ 144,203	$ 15,884	$ 29,723	$ 130,364	$ 22,255

* Payments on bonds and notes payable are made by the debt service fund. The accumulated termination pay and compensated absences liabilities will be liquidated by several of the governmental funds. The claims and judgments liability will generally be liquidated by the workers compensation internal service fund.

also disclose which governmental funds typically have been used to liquidate other long-term liabilities in prior years (Q234).

DETAILED RECONCILIATIONS

Statement 34 requires a reconciliation of the governmental fund statements to the district-wide statements. This reconciliation must be presented on the face of the fund statements or in a schedule following the statement. The balance sheet reconciles fund balance with the net assets of the governmental activities. The statement of revenues, expenditures, and changes in fund balance reconciles net change in fund balance with the change in net assets of governmental activities. More detailed reconciliations may need to be included in the notes to financial statements (see Figures 5-4 and 5-5; Q189, 190, 191 and 218; Appendix 4, Exercise 6). GASB states "if aggregated information in the summary reconciliation obscures the nature of the individual elements of a particular reconciling item, governments should provide a more detailed explanation in the notes to financial statements." ASBO's recommendation regarding a separate reconciliation schedule may preclude the necessity of a detailed note disclosure.

Figure 5-4   Illustrative Note Disclosure Reconciling the Governmental Funds Balance Sheet with the District-Wide Statement of Net Assets.

Note 5—Explanation of Differences between Governmental Funds Balance Sheet and the Statement of Net Assets

"Total fund balances" of the District's governmental funds ($74,630,486) differs from "net assets" of governmental activities ($290,563,158) reported in the statement of net assets. This difference primarily results from the additional long-term economic focus of the statement of net assets versus the solely current financial resources focus of the governmental fund balance sheets.

Balance Sheet/Statement of Net Assets

	Total Governmental Funds	Long-term Assets, Liabilities [a]	Internal Service Funds [b]	Reclassifications and Eliminations	Statement of Net Assets Totals
ASSETS					
Cash and cash equivalents	$ 106,268,980	—	—	—	$ 106,268,980
Property taxes receivable (net)	12,182,730	—	—	—	12,182,730
Due from other governments	19,968,336	—	—	—	19,968,336
Due from other funds	7,782,292	—	$ 17,589,312	$ (24,756,007)	615,597
Other receivables	2,252,919	—	—	—	2,252,919
Inventories and other assets	1,537,230	—	—	—	1,537,230
Capital assets	—	$ 315,524,231	—	—	315,524,231
Total assets	**$ 149,992,487**	**$ 315,524,231**	**$ 17,589,312**	**$ (24,756,007)**	**$ 458,350,023**
LIABILITIES					
Accounts payable and other current liabilities	$ 31,712,117		$ 11,566,721	$ 1,593,237	$ 44,872,075
Due to other funds	26,349,244	—	—	(26,349,244)	0
Matured bonds and interest payable	0				0
Deferred revenue	15,300,640	(12,182,730)	—	—	3,117,910
Long-term liabilities	—	118,796,880	—	—	118,796,880
Total liabilities	**73,362,001**	**106,614,150**	**11,566,721**	**(24,756,007)**	**166,786,865**
FUND BALANCES/NET ASSETS					
Total fund balances/net assets	76,630,486	208,910,081	6,022,591	—	291,563,158
Total liabilities and fund balances/net assets	**$ 149,992,487**	**$ 315,524,231**	**$ 17,589,312**	**$ (24,756,007)**	**$ 458,350,023**

a The costs of building and acquiring capital assets (land, buildings, equipment) financed from the governmental funds are reported as expenditures in the year they are incurred, and the assets do not appear on the balance sheet. However, the statement of net assets includes those capital assets among the assets of the district as a whole, and their original costs are expensed annually over their useful lives.

Original cost of capital assets	$ 413,701,452
Accumulated depreciation	(98,177,221)
	$ 315,524,231

Because the governmental funds focus on short-term financing, some assets will not be available to pay for current-period expenditures. Those assets (for example, receivables) are offset by deferred revenue in the governmental funds and thus are not included in fund balance. They are, however, included in the net assets of the governmental activities.

Adjustment of deferred revenue	$ 12,182,730

Long-term liabilities are reported in the statement of net assets but not in the governmental funds because they are not due and payable in the current period. Balances at June 30, 2002 were:

Bonds and notes payable	$ 101,179,845
Compensated absences	1,125,955
Accumulated termination pay	16,491,080
Subtotal, long-term liabilities	$ 118,796,880

b Internal service funds are used by management to charge the costs of certain activities, such as insurance and telecommunications, to individual funds of the district. The assets and liabilities of the internal service funds, which are reported in the proprietary funds rather than the governmental funds, are included in governmental activities in the statement of net assets.

Figure 5-5 Illustrative Note Disclosure Reconciling the Governmental Funds Statement of Revenues, Expenditures, and Changes in Fund Balances with the District-Wide Statement of Activities.

Note 6—Explanation of Differences between Governmental Funds Operating Statement and the Statement of Activities

Total revenues and other financing sources ($408,174,460) in the governmental funds differ from total revenues for governmental activities ($406,764,735) in the statement of activities. The differences result primarily from the economic focus of the statement of activities versus the current financial resources focus of the governmental funds. The main components of the difference are described below.

Total revenues and other financing sources of the governmental funds consist of:

Revenues	$ 404,880,307
Proceeds from capital leases	692,245
Proceeds from sale of land	2,601,908
Total revenues and other sources—governmental funds	408,174,460

Because some property taxes will not be collected for several months after the District's fiscal year ends, they are not considered as "available" revenues in the governmental funds.

517,087

The proceeds from the sale of land ($2,601,980) are reported as revenue (as a special item) in the governmental funds. However, the cost of the land sold ($1,235,000) is removed from the capital assets account in the statement of net assets and offset against the sale proceeds resulting in a "gain on sale of land'" in the statement of activities. Thus, the revenue reported in the governmental funds is greater than the gain in the statement of activities.

(1,234,567)

Some of the assets acquired this year were financed with capital leases. The amount financed by the leases is reported in the governmental funds as a source of financing. However, capital leases are not revenues in the statement of activities, but long-term liabilities in the statement of net assets.

(692,245)

Total revenues of governmental activities in the statement of activities consist of:

Charges for services	$	8,495,891
Operating grants and contributions		42,270,310
General revenues and special item		355,998,534
Total revenues of governmental activities	$	**406,764,735**

Total expenditures ($391,033,289) of the governmental funds differ from total expenses of governmental activities ($387,689,545) reported in the statement of activities. The difference is attributable primarily to the economic focus of governmental activities versus the current financial resources focus of governmental funds. The main components of the differences are described below.

Total expenditures reported in Governmental Funds

$ **391,033,289**

In the statement of activities, certain operating expenses--compensated absences (vacations) and special termination benefits (early retirement)--are measured by the amounts *earned* during the year. In the governmental funds, however, expenditures for these items are measured by the amount of financial resources used (essentially, the amounts actually *paid*). This year, special termination benefits paid ($10,300,426) *exceeded* the amounts earned ($7,906,074) by $2,394,352. Vacation used ($261,132) was *less than* the amounts earned ($327,280) by $66,148.

(2,328,204)

When the purchase or construction of capital assets is financed through the governmental funds, the resources expended for those assets are reported as expenditures in the years they are incurred. However, in the statement of activities the cost of those assets is allocated over their estimated useful lives and reported as depreciation expense. This is the amount by which depreciation ($13,108,809) exceeded capital expenditures ($930,864) in the current period.

12,177,945

An internal service fund is used by management to charge the costs of unemployment insurance to individual funds. The governmental funds expenditures include the $23,864,586 that the internal service fund charged. The expenses of the governmental activities, however do not reflect the amount paid, but the actual cost of the insurance ($22,639,927). The difference represents an overcharge by the internal service fund that is allocated back to the governmental activities.

(1,224,659)

Repayment of bond principal is an expenditure in the governmental funds, but it reduces long-term liabilities in the statement of net assets and does not affect the statement of activities.

(13,526,946)

Interest on long-term debt in the statement of activities differs from the amount reported in the governmental funds because interest is recorded as an expenditure in the funds when it is due, and thus requires the use of current financial resources. In the statement of activities, however, interest expense is recognized as the interest accrues, regardless of when it is due. The additional interest reported in the statement of activities is the net result of two factors. First, accrued interest on bonds, leases, and contracts payable *decreased* by $43,380. Second, $1,601,500 of additional accumulated interest was accreted on the district's "capital appreciation" bonds.

1,558,120

Total expenses of governmental activities

$ 387,689,545

The notes to the financial statements provide necessary disclosure of material items, the omission of which would cause the financial statements to be misleading. The suggested areas to be considered for notes, as listed above, are neither all-inclusive nor intended to replace the professional judgment of district officials in determining if additional disclosures are necessary. This assessment must be balanced, however, by a desire not to clutter the notes and thereby make them difficult to comprehend.

Chapter Six

The Comprehensive Annual Financial Report

Many school districts publish a Comprehensive Annual Financial Report (CAFR). A CAFR (Q158 and 246) is a district's official annual financial report, containing the basic financial statements as well as introductory material, additional statements and schedules, and other financial, economic and demographic information. The information in the CAFR combining and individual fund statements and schedules is useful to show fund data in more detail than what is presented in the basic financial statements.

Statement 34 does not change the requirements of the (CAFR). Accordingly, the basic CAFR triage of introductory, financial, and statistical sections is still required. The contents of the three sections include:

- Introductory section, including a letter of transmittal
- Financial section, which includes the auditor's report, management's discussion and analysis (MD&A), basic financial statements, required supplemental information (RSI), combining and individual fund financial statements and schedules
- Statistical section

INTRODUCTORY SECTION

The "Introductory Section" is the first major section of a CAFR. As the name implies, this section introduces the reader to the CAFR. It provides an overview of the annual report. It includes the following:

- Cover
- Title Page
- Table of Contents
- Transmittal Letter
- Certificate of Excellence Award (if applicable)
- Listing of Board Members and Administrators
- Organizational Chart

The Transmittal Letter describes the school district's organizational and management structure as well as the general policies and procedures. This letter is important for those who may not read the entire document.

The school district may want to supplement items in the financial statements with other relevant information that is not covered elsewhere in the CAFR. The transmittal letter should not duplicate information that is required to be reported in the MD&A. If the district previously prepared a CAFR, the transmittal letter will need to be modified as a result of Statement 34 so that it will not duplicate the same information. The transmittal letter will still contain information that is not required in the MD&A. It may also compliment, reinforce, and/or reference information that is now reported in the MD&A. The MD&A is considered to be RSI and as such its requirements take precedence over the transmittal letter.

ASBO's Certificate of Excellence (COE) Program (see Appendix C) establishes the following criteria in the ASBO self-evaluation worksheet for the transmittal letter. The transmittal letter should be:

- presented on the letterhead stationery of the school district
- dated on or after the date of the auditor's report
- signed by *both* the chief financial officer and the chief executive officer (may include others at the school's option).

The transmittal letter should include, but not be limited to, discussions of the following subjects:
Management responsibility for financial information

- Explanation of CAFR sections
- Definition of the reporting entity
- Internal controls

- Budgetary controls
- Cash management
- Risk management
- Independent audit with scope limitations discussed
- Certificate of Excellence
- Acknowledgments
- Service Efforts and Accomplishments

The transmittal letter should be consistent with those in the other sections of the CAFR. The COE Award is valid for only one year. Thus, if a school has received the Certificate of Excellence in Financial Reporting for its preceding CAFR, the Introductory Section should include a copy of that year's certificate. The listing of Board Members and Administrators and Organizational Chart can be displayed in any of a number of ways.

FINANCIAL SECTION

The financial section consists of management's discussion and analysis, the auditor's report, the basic financial statements including notes to financial statements, RSI, and the combining and individual fund financial statements, and should include the following:

1. Management's Discussion and Analysis (MD&A) is presented before the basic financial statements. It introduces the basic financial statements and includes an analytical overview of the school district's financial activities (See Chapter 1).
2. Auditor's Opinion Letter.
3. The Basic Financial Statements are the heart of the school district's comprehensive annual financial report, consisting of the district-wide statements, fund statements, and notes to the financial statements.
4. Required Supplementary Information (RSI). Besides the MD&A discussed above, the school district is required to present budgetary comparison schedules, if not presented as a basic statement.
5. Combining and individual fund financial statements and schedules, which consist of the following:

- Combining Statements
  a. By non-major fund, when the school district has more than one non-major fund.
  b. For discretely presented component units, when the reporting entity has more than one component unit (major component units should be presented in the basic statements or notes).
- Individual Fund Statement, when a school district wants to present prior-year and budgetary comparisons.
- Schedules, when a school district wants to present schedules necessary to demonstrate compliance with finance-related legal and contractual provisions or schedules to summarize information presented throughout the statements that can be brought together and shown in greater detail (for example, taxes receivable, including delinquent taxes; long-term debt; investments; cash receipts, disbursements, and balances).

STATISTICAL SECTION

The last section of a CAFR is the "Statistical Section," which presents comparative data for several periods of time, most often ten years. This section may contain data from sources other than the accounting records. These sources should be indicated on each schedule. The use of graphs is beneficial to readers of this section. At a minimum, the COE Program criteria requires the following information in this section of the CAFR:

- District-Wide Revenues and Expenditures—Last 10 Fiscal Years
- General School District Expenditures by Function—Last 10 Fiscal Years
- General School District Revenues by Source—Last 10 Fiscal Years
- Property Tax Levies and Collections—Last 10 Fiscal Years
- Assessed and Estimated Actual Value of Taxable Property—Last 10 Fiscal Years
- Property Tax Rates, All Direct and Overlapping Governments—Last 10 Fiscal Years
- Ratio of Net General Bonded Debt to Assessed Value and Net Bonded Debt per Capita—Last 10 Fiscal Years

- Computation of Legal Debt Margin
- Computation of Direct and Overlapping Debt
- Ratio of Annual Debt Service Expenditures for General Bonded Debt to Total General Expenditures—Last 10 Fiscal Years
- Revenue Bond Coverage—Last 10 Fiscal Years
- Demographic Statistics—Last 10 Fiscal Years
- Property Values, Construction, and Bank Deposits—Last 10 Fiscal Years
- Principal Taxpayers
- Miscellaneous Statistics

Although listed above, the revenue bond coverage tables are not commonly found in school district CAFRs. In addition to the tables listed above, other information may be presented in the Statistical Section. Examples include:

- Annual average FTE
- Student enrollment and attendance data
- Food service operations
- Operational expenditures by pupil
- Per-pupil expenditure ranking
- Schedule of insurance and surety bonds in force

For more information on Financial Reporting and financial statement examples under Statement 34, order "Financial Reporting under GASB Statement No. 34" from ASBO International.

Chapter Seven

Achieving Excellence with Financial Reporting

When selecting a report-writer or report-generator for your GASB Statement 34 financial statements, you should choose one that can produce both current model reports and GASB Statement 34 reports. This ability will become important during the implementation of GASB Statement 34, since you will need to convert last year's current model financial statements to GASB Statement 34 financial statements. Financial Reporting of Governments (F.R.O.G.) report writing software was designed specifically to address the new financial reporting requirements that state and local governments must adhere to under the new reporting model. F.R.O.G. has incredible flexibility as well as the necessary ability to produce reports under both the current and new models. This flexibility is necessary during the transition period of implementation, since many governments will need to prepare financial reports under the current model prior to GASB Statement 34 implementation. F.R.O.G. makes implementation easy, as it allows you to produce your GASB Statement 34 reports once the accrual entries are entered. The effectiveness of F.R.O.G. as an implementation tool has resulted in many school districts deciding to implement the new standard *early.*

F.R.O.G. was developed by the certified public accounting firm of Heinfeld, Meech & Co., P.C. Since its inception in 1986, this firm has specialized in auditing and preparing financial statements for governmental entities. Heinfeld, Meech & Co., P.C. has assisted its clients in obtaining more than 450 Certificates of Excellence from ASBO International. F.R.O.G. has been utilized by the firm and its clients in preparing the reports necessary for these awards, including over thirty GASB 34 implementations.

F.R.O.G. was developed as a result of Heinfeld, Meech & Co., P.C.'s cutting-edge leadership in governmental auditing and consulting. For over four years, F.R.O.G. has been used to prepare financial statements under both the new and old financial reporting models. After receiving feedback from the users of the program, a new version of F.R.O.G. has been developed to include virtually unlimited account code segments, data import and increased report generation flexibility. F.R.O.G. is a self-contained program, therefore there is no need to rely on complicated spreadsheet programs to prepare your financial statements. With all of these features, F.R.O.G. provides the flexibility, reliability and accuracy that results in quality that is unmatched by any other report writing software package designed exclusively for governments.

F.R.O.G. facilitates implementation due to its reliability and ease of use. F.R.O.G. does not replace the familiar as it stores the fund-based information in much the same fashion as your current general ledger. F.R.O.G. allows you to post government-wide journal entries to your fund-based financial data and produce presentation ready financial statements. Finally, F.R.O.G. has been battle tested as it has been used to prepare the financial statements for many entities that have decided to implement the new reporting model early. Most of these entities issued Comprehensive Annual Financial Reports (CAFR) and F.R.O.G. was able to produce all of the financial statements contained within the reports.

The following points highlight the basic features of the F.R.O.G. software.

- F.R.O.G. is a *self-contained*, database-driven, Windows-based program. So it is user-friendly and familiar.
- F.R.O.G.'s toolbar allows quick access to the most frequently used features of the program. This further facilitates and streamlines report preparation time.
- F.R.O.G. enables you to customize the account structure to suit your specific needs. This is accomplished when you initially set up your database structure. However, if you do not want to take the time to customize your account structure, you can copy one of the standard account code structures that come with the program.

- You determine the number of segments that you would like in your account structure. These segments can include, but are not limited to: *Fund, Department, Program, Function and Object.*
- Upon deciding on the number of segments you want, you can begin to set up the segment codes. This is when you would set up your fund, program, department, function and object codes.
- Once you have set up all of the codes needed for your segments, you are ready to take the next step of setting up your *account code structure*, by fund. This is the point where your F.R.O.G. software begins to look similar to the account code structure in a general ledger package.
- Once you have created the accounts for a particular fund, F.R.O.G. enables you to clone funds so that you may copy similar fund types (e.g., General, Special Revenue, Debt Service, etc.) and save time setting up fund account structures.
- Now you are ready to load the data from your general ledger using the quick data entry screen or data upload function.
- Once your general ledger data is in F.R.O.G., you are able to make adjustments to your fund financial information using the journal entry screen and your government-wide adjustments using the government-wide journal entry screen.
- After all of your adjustments are made, you are now ready to print your reports. With a click of a button you will have presentation-ready financial statements. It is that easy and it is no wonder why the number of users of F.R.O.G. increase every day.

To test out the many features of F.R.O.G. for yourself, visit the official F.R.O.G. website at www.frogonline.net.

Chapter Eight

GAO New Independence Standard

The United States General Accounting Office (GAO) issued a new Government Auditing Standards Amendment No. 3 Independence (GAO-02-3886) in January 2002 due to the issues surrounding Enron, WorldCom, Tyco, Adelphia, Qwest, and Arthur Anderson. As the Sarbanes-Oxley Act of 2002 issued new requirements for SEC clients, the GAO likewise issued this new Independence Standard for governmental entities. In addition to the new standard, the GAO issued "Answers to Independence Standard Questions" in July 2002 (GAO-02-8706). You can download the independence standard and its question and answer guide at www.gao .gov.

The Second General Standard of Government Auditing Standards states "In all matters relating to the audit work, the audit organization and the individual auditor, whether government or public, should be free both in fact and appearance from personal, external, and organizational impairments to independence."

Personal impairments result from relationships or beliefs that might cause the auditor to limit the work performed or weaken or slant audit findings. Examples of personal impairments:

- An immediate or close family member who is an officer of the audit entity, or who can exert direct influence over the audit entity
- A direct or significant indirect financial interest in the audited entity
- Managing or decision-making responsibility for operations within the audited entity

- Performing an audit when currently or previously maintaining official accounting records
- Preconceived ideas regarding the audited entity
- Political or social biases
- Seeking employment with an audit entity during the audit engagement

External impairments result from situations that restrict or interfere with the auditor's ability to gather evidence or form conclusions. Examples of external impairments include:

- Interference or influence that could improperly limit the scope of the auditor's work
- Interference with respect to the auditor's application of audit procedures or selections of transactions to test
- Unreasonable restrictions on the time allowed to complete the audit
- Interference in the auditor's assignment or promotion of audit personnel
- Restricting monies or resources provided to the audit organization
- Authority to overrule or influence auditor's judgment in reporting
- Threatening to replace the auditor over disagreements with audit report contents
- Influence to remove the auditor organization for reasons other than auditor incompetence or misconduct, or new contracts for audit services

Organizational impairments result from government audit organizations that are not properly structured within their government. (This relates to Federal and State auditors.) Government audit organizations are independent to report externally when:

- They are assigned to a different level or branch of government than the audited entity.
- The head of a government audit organization is elected or appointed by and reports to the legislative body.
- They meet similar criteria established in statutes.

Internal audit organizations are independent to report internally to management when the audit head:

- Is accountable to and reports directly to the entity head (or deputy).
- Is located outside the staff or line management function.

For nonaudit services the auditors must carefully consider whether to provide nonaudit services to entities to avoid situations that can impair their independence (in fact or appearance), when they also perform audits of those entities.

The GAO recognizes that audit organizations have the capability of performing a range of services for their clients. *(However, for audits that are required to be conducted under Government Auditing Standards, in certain circumstances it is not appropriate for an audit organization to perform both audit and selected nonaudit services for the same client. In these circumstances, an audit organization and/or an audited entity will have to make a choice as to which of these services an audit organization will provide.)*

Before an auditor agrees to also perform nonaudit services, that auditor must consider the two overarching principles:

- *Do not perform management functions or make management decisions.*
- *Do not audit your own work.*

Auditors may perform nonaudit services that do not violate the two principles if they also comply with the seven safeguards. The seven safeguards regarding nonaudit services are:

- Documenting the rationale that the nonaudit service does not violate the two overarching principles.
- Establishing and documenting an understanding with the audited entity regarding the nonaudit service and each party's responsibility before providing the service.
- Not allowing personnel who provide the nonaudit service to plan, conduct, or review related audit work.

- Not reducing the scope or extent of audit work below the level that would be appropriate if another party provided the nonaudit service.
- Including in the auditor's quality control system, policies and procedures to assure consideration of the effect of the nonaudit service on current and future audits, and documentation of the understanding reached with the audited entity.
- Informing management that by providing the nonaudit service, the auditor can no longer perform the related audit.
- Providing required documentation of nonaudit services to peer review team for audits selected.

Due to the above, many auditors are electing to perform either the audit or nonaudit services.

COMMON ACCEPTABLE NONAUDIT SERVICES

Auditors are still allowed to provide routine advice, technical assistance, training, tools, and best practices, as the decision to follow that advice remains with the management of the audited entity. The standard also provides examples of common nonaudit services that are acceptable as long as auditors do not violate the overarching principles and follow the safeguards.

The GAO's *Government Auditing Standards: Answers to Independence Standard Questions* (June 2002) issued 92 questions. A few of the questions that affect your financial statements are listed below:

1. As related to nonaudit services, what would constitute a management function? This question can best be responded to by illustrating several types of situations that would typically constitute management functions. These include:
   - serving as a member of an entity's management decision-making committee or on its board of directors (although participating as an observer or nonvoting ex-officio member is permitted under paragraph 3.23),
   - making policy decisions affecting the direction and operations of entity programs,

- supervising entity employees,
- developing entity programmatic policies
- authorizing entity transactions, or
- maintaining custody of entity assets (Question 34, pages 26–27).

2. Paragraph 3.26a of the independence standard states that independence is impaired if the audit organization maintains or prepares an audited entity's basic accounting records or maintains or takes responsibility for basic financial or other records that an audit organization will audit. What is considered to be an entity's basic accounting records and basic financial or other records?

Basic accounting and financial records are considered to be source documents or originating data evidencing transactions have occurred (for example, purchase orders, payroll time records, and customer orders). Such records would also include an audited entity's general ledger and subsidiary records, or equivalent. Supporting schedules are not considered to be basic accounting or financial records, as long as management has made all the decisions in key areas regarding these supporting schedules. An example of a supporting schedule is a depreciation schedule (Question 48, pages 39–40).

3. Can an audit organization assist an audited entity's management in preparing depreciation schedules without impairing its independence to perform the financial statement audit?

Yes, as long as the audited entity's management has determined such key factors as the method and rate of depreciation and the salvage value of the assets. If the audit organization makes these decisions, it has violated an overarching principle. To not impair its independence, the audit organization's service must be limited to calculating the depreciation, and the audited entity's management must take responsibility for the depreciation schedules. The audit organization must take care that the extent of its work does not cross the line and place it in a position where reasonable third parties with knowledge of the relevant facts and circumstances could conclude that the auditor's independence is impaired. Also, given the nature of this nonaudit service, the audit organization would not have to apply the safeguard precluding personnel who provided the nonaudit services from auditing their own work. However, the remaining safeguards in paragraph 3.25 would apply (Question 49, page 40).

4. If the audit organization posts transactions coded by the audited entity's management, would the audit organization's independence be impaired to perform the financial statement audit?

Yes. Paragraph 3.26a specifically addresses the posting transactions, whether coded by management or not, to an entity's financial records or to other records that subsequently provide data to an entity's financial records. An audit organization cannot provide this service without impairing its independence to perform the financial statement audit (Question 50, pages 40–41).

5. An audited entity asks an audit organization to assist with implementing GASB Statement No. 34, *Basic Financial Statements—and Management's Discussion and Analysis—for State and Local Governments*. Would an audit organization's independence be impaired?

It would depend on the nature of the assistance provided. GASB Statement No. 34 significantly changed the state and local governmental financial reporting model by redefining the general-purpose external financial statements and by requiring a new section on Management's Discussion and Analysis and that all capital assets, including infrastructure assets, be reported in the financial statements. An audit organization could provide the type of services covered under the independence standard in paragraph 3.23—such as providing routine advice, explaining technical requirements, and providing training—without impairing its independence. Generally, such assistance relating to an audit organization's knowledge and skills would be considered routine and not impair audit independence. However, if an audit organization is asked to perform work that goes beyond routine advice, this work needs to be considered in light of the overarching principles and the safeguards. This would be the case, for example, if an audit organization were asked to perform extensive valuation services, such as may be related to an audited entity's infrastructure assets or to prepare an audited entity's Management's Discussion and Analysis (Question 55, pages 44–45).

6. If an audited entity does not have an internal audit operation and engages an audit organization to perform internal audit services,

would the audit organization's independence be impaired to also serve as the external auditor?

Yes. Internal audit is considered a management function and, for external audit organizations, would impair independence by violating an overarching principle. This would impair the independence of external audit organizations to perform not only the entity's financial statement audit but also performance audits (Question 66, page 54).

7. What if the audit organization instead is asked to recommend individuals for a particular position?

The audit organization can suggest individuals for the audited entity to contact for consideration without impairing the audit organization's independence as long as it provides more than one name for a particular position. However, as discussed in paragraph 3.26f, if an auditor organization recommends a single individual for a specific key position or conducts an executive search or recruiting program for an audited entity, the audit organization's independence would be impaired (Question 92, page 67).

8. Can an audit organization be involved in preparing a trial balance and draft financial statements and notes without impairing its independence to audit the financial statements? Can audit engagement team members perform these activities?

Maintaining the audited entity's books and records is the responsibility of its management. Accordingly, management is responsible for ensuring that these books and records adequately support the preparation of financial statements in accordance with generally accepted accounting principles and that records are current and in balance. . . . The audit organization must be careful not to make management decisions, and management of the audited entity must have the knowledge to evaluate and approve the draft financial statements and notes and take responsibility for them. . . . Likewise, auditors can convert cash-based financial statements to accrual-based financial statements, as long as management is in the position to make informed judgments to review, approve, and take responsibility for the appropriateness of the conversion. . . . It is important to reiterate that the answer to this question is conditioned on the audit organization starting with appropriate books and records that balance and the audited entity having knowledgeable management.

CONCLUSION

Examples of common acceptable nonaudit services include:

- Preparing draft financial statements and notes, schedules, and trial balances, based on the audited entity's chart of accounts and records if management has the knowledge to include and approve the draft financial statements and take responsibility for them;
- Calculating payroll and generating checks for the audited entity, based on the entity's records and data;
- Limiting appraisal and valuation services to reviewing the work of the entity or its specialists;
- Preparing indirect cost proposals or cost allocation plans based on the audited entity's assumptions and data;
- Giving advice on information technology, including system design, installation, and security, as long as the auditor does not design, install, operate (or supervise) the system;
- Evaluating potential candidates for the audited entity, as long as the auditor does not recommend a single individual or search for the candidate;
- Preparing routine tax filings;
- Gathering unverified data to aid legislative or administrative decisions;
- Giving advice about an audited entity's internal control self-assessments; and
- Developing questions for a legislative body for use at hearings.

Perhaps the first question an auditor should ask in this situation is: "Does management have the ability to correctly prepare a trial balance that will lead to a financial statement?" If the answer to this is "NO" then the auditor must acknowledge that management cannot understand and take responsibility for the entries and/or the financial statements. In this situation the auditor may well be making management decisions and auditing the auditor's own work, which according to the new standard would impair independence.

In order to adhere to the GAO New Independence Standard, many firms are performing bookkeeping services, including the preparation of financial statements and audit working papers for the auditors, leaving other firms to perform the audit only.

Appendix A

Sample Management Discussion and Analysis

(Modified from GASB School District User Guide)

This section of ASBO, International School District's (LISD) annual financial report presents our discussion and analysis of the District's financial performance during the fiscal year that ended on June 30, 2002. Please read it in conjunction with the transmittal letter at the front of this report and the District's financial statements, which immediately follow this section.

FINANCIAL HIGHLIGHTS

- The District's financial status improved substantially for the second year in a row. Total net assets increased more than 7 percent over the course of the year.
- Overall revenues were $430 million, fully $20 million more than expenses.
- The total cost of basic programs rose 2.3 percent to $388 million. Because the portion of those costs paid for with charges, fees, and intergovernmental aid increased, the *net* cost that required taxpayer funding grew just 1.2 percent to $337 million.
- The net assets of our business-type activities—food services and adult education—increased more than 11 percent. Revenues

increased 15 percent to $24 million while expenses increased 11 percent to $22 million.

- Food services began a much-needed modernization this year, adding $1,600,000 of new equipment and furniture.
- Enrollment in the vocational and high school equivalency programs increased 12 percent to its highest level ever. The tuition-based continuing education course offerings doubled to 25.
- Outlays for new capital assets were very low because the planned opening of two new school buildings was postponed until next year due to construction delays. Maintenance and operations spending also was significantly below budget as a result.
- The District reduced its outstanding long-term debt $13 million or 11 percent.

OVERVIEW OF THE FINANCIAL STATEMENTS

This annual report consists of three parts—management's discussion and analysis (this section), the basic financial statements, and required supplementary information. The basic financial statements include two kinds of statements that present different views of the District:

- The first two statements are *district-wide financial statements* that provide both *short-term* and *long-term* information about the District's *overall* financial status.
- The remaining statements are *fund financial statements* that focus on *individual parts* of the District, reporting the District's operations in *more detail* than the district-wide statements.
- The *governmental funds* statements tell how *basic* services like regular and special education were financed in the *short term* as well as what remains for future spending.
- *Proprietary funds* statements offer *short-* and *long-term* financial information about the activities the district operates *like businesses*, such as food services.
- *Fiduciary funds* statements provide information about the financial relationships in which the District acts solely as a *trustee or agent* for the benefit of others.

The financial statements also include *notes* that explain some of the information in the statements and provide more detailed data. The statements are followed by a section of *required supplementary information* that further explains and supports the financial statements with a comparison of the District's budget for the year. Figure A-1 shows how the various parts of this annual report are arranged and related to one another.

Figure A-2 summarizes the major features of the District's financial statements, including the portion of the District's activities they cover and the types of information they contain. The remainder of this overview section of management's discussion and analysis highlights the structure and contents of each of the statements.

Figure A-1   Organization of ASBO's Annual Financial Report.

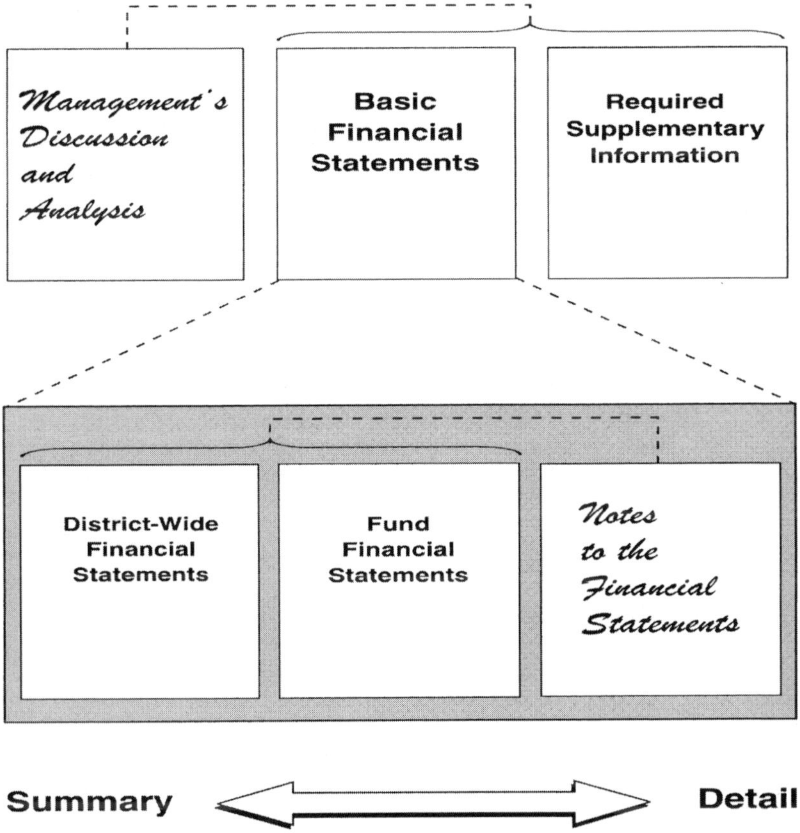

Figure A-2 Major Features of the District-Wide and Fund Financial Statements.

	District-wide Statements	Fund Financial Statements		
		Governmental Funds	Proprietary Funds	Fiduciary Funds
Scope	Entire district (except fiduciary funds)	The activities of the district that are not proprietary or fiduciary, such as special education and building maintenance	Activities the district operates similar to private businesses: food services and adult education	Instances in which the district administers resources on behalf of someone else, such as scholarship programs and student activities monies
Required financial statements	• Statement of net assets • Statement of activities	• Balance sheet • Statement of revenues, expenditures, and changes in fund balances	• Statement of net assets • Statement of revenues, expenses, and changes in fund net assets • Statement of cash flows	• Statement of fiduciary net assets • Statement of changes in fiduciary net assets
Accounting basis and measurement focus	Accrual accounting and economic resources focus	Modified accrual accounting and current financial resources focus	Accrual accounting and economic resources focus	Accrual accounting and economic resources focus
Type of asset/liability information	All assets and liabilities, both financial and capital, short-term and long-term	Generally assets expected to be used up and liabilities that come due during the year or soon thereafter; no capital assets or long-term liabilities included	All assets and liabilities, both financial and capital, and short-term and long-term	All assets and liabilities, both short-term and long-term; Luna's funds do not currently contain capital assets, although they can
Type of inflow/outflow information	All revenues and expenses during year, regardless of when cash is received or paid	Revenues for which cash is received during or soon after the end of the year; expenditures when goods or services have been received and the related liability is due and payable	All revenues and expenses during the year, regardless of when cash is received or paid	All additions and deductions during the year, regardless of when cash is received or paid

DISTRICT-WIDE STATEMENTS

The district-wide statements report information about the District as a whole using accounting methods similar to those used by private-sector companies. The statement of net assets includes *all* of the District's assets and liabilities. All of the current year's revenues and expenses are accounted for in the statement of activities regardless of when cash is received or paid.

The two district-wide statements report the District's *net assets* and how they have changed. Net assets—the difference between the District's assets and liabilities—is one way to measure the District's financial health or *position.*

- Over time, increases or decreases in the District's net assets are an indicator of whether its financial position is improving or deteriorating, respectively.
- To assess the overall health of the District you need to consider additional non-financial factors such as changes in the District's property tax base and the condition of school buildings and other facilities.

In the district-wide financial statements, the District's activities are divided into two categories:

- *Governmental activities*—Most of the District's basic services are included here, such as regular and special education, transportation, and administration. Property taxes and state formula aid finance most of these activities.
- *Business-type activities*—The District charges fees to help it cover the costs of certain services it provides. The District's adult education programs and food services are included here.

FUND FINANCIAL STATEMENTS

The fund financial statements provide more detailed information about the District's *funds,* focusing on its most significant or "major" funds— not the District as a whole. Funds are accounting devices the District uses to keep track of specific sources of funding and spending on particular programs:

- Some funds are required by State law and by bond covenants.
- The District establishes other funds to control and manage money for particular purposes (like repaying its long-term debts) or to show that it is properly using certain revenues (like federal grants).

The District has three kinds of funds:

- *Governmental funds*—Most of the District's basic services are included in governmental funds, which generally focus on (1) how *cash and other financial assets* that can readily be converted to cash flow in and out and (2) the balances left at year-end that are available for spending. Consequently, the governmental funds statements provide a detailed *short-term* view that helps you determine whether there are more or fewer financial resources that can be spent in the near future to finance the District's programs. Because this information does not encompass the additional long-term focus of the district-wide statements, we provide additional information at the bottom of the governmental funds statements that explains the relationship (or differences) between them.
- *Proprietary funds*—Services for which the District charges a fee are generally reported in proprietary funds. Proprietary funds are reported in the same way as the district-wide statements. In fact, the District's *enterprise funds* (one type of proprietary fund) are the same as its business-type activities, but provide more detail and additional information, such as cash flows. We use *internal service funds* (the other kind of proprietary fund) to report activities that provide supplies and services for the District's other programs and activities. The district currently has one internal service fund—the workers' compensation fund.
- *Fiduciary funds*—The District is the trustee, or *fiduciary,* for assets that belong to others, such as the scholarship fund and the student activities funds. The District is responsible for ensuring that the assets reported in these funds are used only for their intended purposes and by those to whom the assets belong. We exclude these

activities from the district-wide financial statements because the District cannot use these assets to finance its operations.

FINANCIAL ANALYSIS OF THE DISTRICT AS A WHOLE

Net Assets

The District's *combined* net assets were significantly larger on June 30, 2002, than they were the year before—increasing more than 7 percent to $304.0 million. (See Figure A-3.) Most of this improvement in the District's financial position came from its governmental activities, the net assets of which grew $19.1 million to $291.6 million. The net assets of the District's business-type activities increased $1.3 million to $12.4 million; while the dollar growth was smaller, it nonetheless represented an increase of more than 11 percent.

The District's improved financial position is the product of many factors. Growth during the year in taxes and grants was a significant contributor to this improvement. Another notable factor was a construction workers strike that delayed the planned opening of two new school buildings—Common Middle School and Basic High School for the Arts—until next year. Consequently, about $2 million of expected maintenance and operations costs related to the new buildings did not arise.

Changes in Net Assets

The District's total revenues (excluding a special item) increased 4 percent to $429.1 million. (See Figure A-4.) Property taxes and state formula aid accounted for most of the District's revenue, with each contributing about 40 cents of every dollar raised. (See Figure A-5.) Another 14 percent came from state and federal aid for specific programs, and the remainder from fees charged for services and miscellaneous sources.

The total cost of all programs and services rose 2.7 percent to $410.1 million. The District's expenses are predominantly related to instructing, caring for (pupil services) and transporting students (74 percent). (See Figure A-6.) The administrative and business activities of the District accounted for 11 percent of total costs. The most significant contributor

Figure A-3   Condensed Statement of Net Assets (in Millions of Dollars).

	Governmental Activities		Business-type Activities		Total School District		Total Percentage Change
	2001	2002	2001	2002	2001	2002	2001–2002
Current and other assets	$117.8	$142.8	$ 9.9	$11.2	$127.7	$154.0	20.6%
Capital assets	329.1	315.5	1.9	2.5	331.0	318.1	–3.9%
Total assets	**446.9**	**458.4**	**11.8**	**13.7**	**458.7**	**472.1**	**2.9%**
Long-term debt outstand	134.0	118.8	—	—	134.0	118.8	–11.3%
Other liabilities	40.4	48.0	0.7	1.3	41.1	49.3	20.0%
Total liabilities	174.4	166.8	0.7	1.3	175.1	168.1	–4.0%
Net assets							
Invested in capital assets, net of related debt	219.2	231.1	1.9	2.5	221.1	233.7	5.7%
Restricted	6.0	5.5	—	—	6.0	5.5	–7.5%
Unrestricted	47.3	54.9	9.2	9.9	56.6	64.8	14.5%
Total net assets	**$272.5**	**$291.6**	**$11.1**	**$12.4**	**$283.6**	**$304.0**	**7.2%**

Note: totals may not add due to rounding.

Figure A-4 Changes in Net Assets from Operating Results (in Millions of Dollars).

	Governmental Activities		Business-type Activities		Total School District		Total Percentage Change
	2001	2002	2001	2002	2001	2002	2001–2002
Revenues							
Program revenues							
Charges for services	$ 7.9	$ 8.5	$ 5.0	$ 5.7	$ 12.9	$ 14.2	10.2%
Operating Grants & Contributions	38.3	42.3	15.3	17.0	53.7	59.3	10.4%
Capital Grants & Contributions				0.7	—	0.7	
General revenues							
Property taxes	162.8	171.0	—	—	162.8	171.0	5.0%
State formula aid	175.0	176.3	—	—	175.0	176.3	0.7%
Other	6.8	7.4	0.3	0.3	7.0	7.7	9.5%
Total revenues	**390.8**	**405.4**	**20.6**	**23.7**	**411.4**	**429.1**	**4.3%**
Expenses							
Instruction	228.9	234.8			228.9	234.8	2.6%
Pupil & Instructional Services	44.8	44.0			44.8	44.0	−1.8%
Administration & Business	43.7	41.4			43.7	41.4	−5.3%
Maintenance & operations	29.5	30.4			29.5	30.4	3.1%
Transportation	8.8	8.6			8.8	8.6	−2.3%
Other	23.4	28.5	20.2	22.4	43.6	50.9	16.7%
Total expenses	**379.1**	**387.7**	**20.2**	**22.4**	**399.3**	**410.1**	**2.7%**
Excess (deficiency) before special item	11.7	17.7	0.4	1.3	12.1	19.0	56.9%
Special item: land sale	—	1.4				1.4	—
Increase (decrease) in net asset:	**$ 11.7**	**$ 19.1**	**$ 0.4**	**$ 1.3**	**$ 12.1**	**$ 20.4**	**68.2%**

Note: totals may not add due to rounding.

Figure A-5   Sources of Revenue for Fiscal Year 2002.

Other
2%

Property taxes
40%

State formula aid
41%

Federal & state
categorical
grants
14%

Charges for
services
3%

to the higher costs was maintenance and operations expenses, which increased $900,000 or 3.1 percent, due primarily to salary increases for custodial and security personnel and higher fuel costs due to a particularly cold winter. The $6.0 million increase in instructional costs also derives largely from salary increases, in this case for teachers and other educational staff.

Total revenues (including the gain from an unused lot the district sold) surpassed expenses, increasing net assets $20.4 million over last year. Both the governmental and business-type activities contributed to the District's healthier fiscal status.

Figure A-6   Expenses for Fiscal Year 2002.

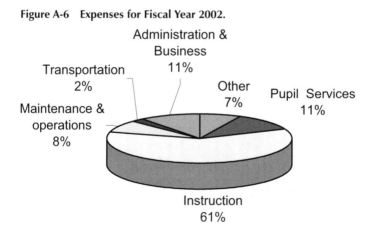

Administration &
Business
11%

Transportation
2%

Other
7%

Pupil Services
11%

Maintenance &
operations
8%

Instruction
61%

Governmental Activities

Revenues for the District's governmental activities (excluding the land sale) increased 3.7 percent, while total expenses increased 2.3 percent. With the gain on the sale of the land, the increase in net assets for governmental activities was $19.1 million in 2002. This was the second consecutive year that net assets increased substantially, following an $11.7 million increase in 2001.

The recent good health of the District's finances can be credited both to a strong economy and innovative management changes:

- Rising real estate values led to a 5 percent increase in property tax revenues, despite the fact that tax rates remained unchanged. The District has not raised tax rates since 1997. Operating grants and contributions for governmental activities increased 10.4 percent to $42.3 million.

- The District sold a vacant parcel of land for $2.6 million, for a gain (net of the $1.2 million originally paid) of $1.4 million. The District originally purchased the land in 1988 as a site for a new school to replace Common Middle School's aging building. The District ultimately decided to construct the new school nearby on Common's current campus. Although the District did not need the proceeds from the sale to finance services this year, the decision to sell the land this year was based on the availability of a buyer and the District's judgment that a better offer was not likely to be received in the near future. This sale was a one-time occurrence—the District has no further plans to sell other assets, and therefore future budgets will not count on these resources recurring.

- The District is in the second year of implementing the Superintendent's Efficiency and Effectiveness Plan. The goal of the SEE Plan is to initiate changes that reduce the cost of operating the District and reinvest the savings in programs to modernize and raise the quality of education. The actions taken thus far include:

  - Redrawing bus routes to reduce the total number of routes and buses needed.
  - Shifting non-pedagogical personnel to free teachers from administrative tasks.

- Contracting out some services previously provided to individual schools by the central District office.

These actions resulted in savings of approximately $3 million in 2002. The District will begin to use these savings in 2003 for projects agreed upon by a committee of school-based and central District teaching, support, supervisory, and administrative personnel.

Figure A-7 presents the cost of six major District activities: instruction, pupil and instructional services, administration and business, maintenance and operations, transportation, and other. The table also shows each activity's *net cost* (total cost less fees generated by the activities and intergovernmental aid provided for specific programs). The net cost shows the financial burden that was placed on the District's taxpayers by each of these functions.

- The cost of all *governmental* activities this year was $387.7 million.
- Some of the cost was financed by the users of the District's programs ($8.5 million).
- The federal and state governments subsidized certain programs with grants and contributions ($42.3 million).
- Most of the District's costs ($336.9 million), however, were financed by District taxpayers and the taxpayers of our state.
- This portion of governmental activities was financed with $171.0 million in property taxes, $176.3 million of unrestricted state aid based on the statewide education aid formula, and with investment earnings.

Business-Type Activities

Revenues of the District's business-type activities increased 15.0 percent to $23.7 million and expenses rose 10.9 percent to $22.4 million. (Refer to Figure A-4.) Factors contributing to these results included:

- Food services revenues exceeded expenses by $1.1 million, accounting for most of the increase in the net assets of the business-type activities. At the start of the school year in September 2001 food services raised prices 5 percent across the board with the intention of

Figure A-7 Net Cost of Governmental Activities (in Millions of Dollars).

| | Total Cost of Services | | Percentage Change | Net Cost of Services | | Percentage Change |
	2001	2002	2001–2002	2001	2002	2001–2002
Instruction	$228.9	$234.8	2.6%	$197.3	$201.6	2.2%
Pupil & Instructional Services	44.8	44.0	−1.8%	36.3	36.3	−0.6%
Administration & Business	43.7	41.4	−5.3%	39.2	36.8	−6.1%
Maintenance & operations	29.5	30.4	3.1%	26.7	27.5	3.0%
Transportation	8.8	8.6	−2.3%	7.6	7.8	2.6%
Other	23.4	28.5	21.8%	25.7	27.1	5.4%
Total	**$379.1**	**$387.7**	**2.3%**	**$332.8**	**$336.9**	**1.2%**

Note: totals may not add due to rounding.

building resources to replace and modernize its old and obsolete kitchen equipment. The District also received a state capital grant of $750,000 to help defray the modernization costs. During the year $1,600,000 of new equipment and furniture was purchased, and additional purchases will be made next year using the surplus resources from this year.

- The adult education program was dramatically expanded in 2002.
- The grant-supported high school equivalency and vocational training courses served 3,500 adults, up 12 percent from the prior year and the highest enrollment since the program's inception.
- The number of tuition-based continuing education courses doubled from 12 to 25, with a total enrollment of nearly 900 for the year.

FINANCIAL ANALYSIS OF THE DISTRICT'S FUNDS

The strong financial performance of the District as a whole is reflected in its governmental funds as well. As the District completed the year, its governmental funds reported *combined* fund balances of $76.6 million, well above last year's ending fund balances of $59.5 million.

All but one of the District's governmental funds had more revenues than expenditures in 2002, thereby contributing to the increase in total fund balance. Most significantly, $3.5 million of planned capital outlays connected with the opening of two new schools did not take place because of a construction strike. The only fund that ran a deficit was the family assistance fund, a special revenue fund that records the use of block grant money received from the state for providing parenting and counseling services to the parents of disadvantaged students. Expenditures of that fund were approximately $658,000 above revenues because some unused resources from last year were used this year to finance expenditures.

As mentioned, the business-type activities also did well financially. In addition to the district-wide financial statements, food services and the adult education program are reported in greater detail in the enterprise funds statements. In 2002 both services took steps that were important to District finances:

- Enrollment in the adult education courses grew rapidly, especially among the courses that charge a fee to participants. This growth has an impact on the governmental funds, because the program pays the District for the classroom and administrative space it utilizes. In 2002 the program's facility rental cost was $827,000.
- The equipment used by food services is old and, in some cases, obsolete. Despite adding $1.6 million of new equipment and furnishings in 2002, food services' capital assets were 78 percent depreciated. A 5 percent price increase on all menu items was enacted as part of an effort to raise the resources necessary to modernize and replace the old equipment, and the state provided a grant of $750,000.

General Fund Budgetary Highlights

Over the course of the year, the District revised the annual operating budget several times. These budget amendments fall into two categories:

- Changes made in the third and fourth quarters to account for the postponed opening of two new school facilities and for higher-than-expected property tax revenues.
- Increases in appropriations to prevent budget overruns.

While the District's final budget for the general fund anticipated that revenues and expenditures would be roughly equal, the actual results for the year show a $13.6 million surplus.

- Actual revenues were $3.6 million higher than expected, due largely to the property tax and some unexpected state aid.
- The actual expenditures were $9.9 million below budget, due primarily to the delayed opening of the new school buildings:
- Budgeted capital outlays of $5.1 million were actually $923,000 for the year; virtually all of the difference is accounted for by the final payments on the school construction.
- Actual expenditures for maintenance and operations of school facilities were more than $2.0 million below budgeted levels.

CAPITAL ASSET AND DEBT ADMINISTRATION

Capital Assets

By the end of 2002 the District had invested $318 million in a broad range of capital assets, including school buildings, athletic facilities, computer and audio-visual equipment, and administrative offices. (See Figure A-8.) This amount represents a net decrease of $13 million or 3.9 percent from last year. (More detailed information about capital assets can be found in Note 2 to the financial statements.) Total depreciation expense for the year exceeded $14 million and land originally costing $1.3 million was sold, while building improvements and additions to equipment and furniture amounted to just $2.5 million.

The District had expected to complete the two school buildings this year, but construction difficulties have delayed their opening until next year. ASBO's student enrollment has grown steadily over the last three years—9 percent since 1999 to reach a present enrollment of 73,650. Since 1996 student enrollment has exceeded the District's seating capacity. When complete, the two state-of-the-art school facilities will provide 7,000 additional seats, bringing the District's capacity to nearly 75,000.

The District's fiscal year 2003 capital budget projects spending another $6 million for capital projects, principally in two areas:

- $4 million to complete the new facilities for Common Middle School and Basic High School.
- $1.5 million to continue the modernization of the food service equipment.

Long-Term Debt

At year-end the District had $101 million in general obligation bonds and other long-term debt outstanding—a reduction of 11 percent from last year—as shown in Figure A-9. (More detailed information about the District's long-term liabilities is presented in Note 2 to the financial statements.)

- The District continued to pay down its debt, retiring $13.5 million of outstanding bonds.

Figure A-8   Capital Assets (Net of Depreciation, in Millions of Dollars).

	Governmental Activities		Business-type Activities		Total School District		Total Percentage Change
	2001	2002	2001	2002	2001	2002	2001–2002
Land	$ 22.1	$ 20.8	—	—	$ 22.1	$ 20.8	– 5.6%
Construction in progress	11.4	11.4	—	—	11.4	11.4	0.4%
Buildings	188.5	177.9	—	—	188.5	177.9	– 5.7%
Equipment & furniture	106.9	105.4	$1.9	$2.5	108.8	107.9	– 0.9%
Total	$329.0	$315.5	$1.9	$2.5	$330.9	$318.1	– 3.9%

Note: totals may not add due to rounding.

Figure A-9   Outstanding Long-Term Debt (in Millions of Dollars).

	Total School District		Total Percentage Group
	2001	*2002*	*2001–2002*
General obligation bonds & note (financed with property taxes)	$108.2	$96.5	− 10.8%
Other general obligation debt	5.8	4.7	− 19.0%
Total	$114.0	$101.2	− 11.2%

- Only $692,000 in new debt was issued during the year.

The District plans to issue about $4 million in new bonds in 2003 to pay for the completion of the new school buildings. The District will continue to pay cash, however, for the additional food services equipment rather than finance the equipment with long-term debt.

FACTORS BEARING ON
THE DISTRICT'S FUTURE

At the time these financial statements were prepared and audited, the District was aware of four existing circumstances that could significantly affect its financial health in the future:

- The end of fiscal year 2002 marked the expiration of the last three-year teachers contract. A new three-year labor agreement was approved in August 2002. The economic package (salaries and fringe benefits) contained in the new contract provides for 4 percent annual increases. This contract will increase the District's costs $6.6 million in 2003, $13.5 million in 2004, and $20.7 million in 2005.
- The District is plaintiff with other urban school districts in a lawsuit against the state, seeking to rectify inequities in the formula the state uses to apportion education aid to the districts. The District is requesting an additional $40 million of state aid annually.
- The District was a defendant in a lawsuit brought by one of its largest taxpayers. Spehr Tire, Inc. consolidated its manufacturing operations

in its main factory in another state and closed its local plant. The company asked that the assessed value of the now-empty factory be cut drastically to reflect that the property is no longer being used and, Spehr contended, is not capable of generating income for the company. The court decided in favor of Spehr, costing the District about $4 million in annual property tax revenues.

- In 2004 the District must implement the more stringent academic standards mandated by the State Education Board's Total Educational Accountability Reforms (TEARs). TEARs may result in a smaller percentage of students being promoted to the next grade each year and a lower percentage of students graduating from high school. If this were to occur, the District's pupil enrollment would rise. It is not possible at this time to predict what will happen if promotion and graduation rates decline but, based on current costs, every 1 percent enrollment increase would raise instructional costs approximately $2 million annually, not including the cost of support services, transportation, and administration.

CONTACTING THE DISTRICT'S FINANCIAL MANAGEMENT

This financial report is designed to provide our citizens, taxpayers, customers, and investors and creditors with a general overview of the District's finances and to demonstrate the District's accountability for the money it receives. If you have questions about this report or need additional financial information, contact the Controller's Office, ASBO, International School District, 14 Pavilion Road, Reston, VA 22090.

Appendix B

Sunnyside Unified School District No. 12's Management's Discussion and Analysis (MD&A)

As management of the Sunnyside Unified School District No. 12 (District), we offer readers of the District's financial statements this narrative overview and analysis of the financial activities of the District for the fiscal year ended June 30, 2002. We encourage readers to consider the information presented here in conjunction with additional information that we have furnished in our letter of transmittal, which can be found on pages i–v of this report.

FINANCIAL HIGHLIGHTS

- The District's total net assets of governmental activities increased $3.9 million which represents a 8.3 percent increase from fiscal year 2001 was primarily a result of $2.3 million of State funding for capital additions and improvements in the current year.
- General revenues accounted for $84.9 million in revenue, or 82.7 percent of all fiscal year 2002 revenues. Program specific revenues in the form of charges for services and grants and contributions accounted for $17.8 million or 17.3 percent of total fiscal year 2002 revenues.
- The District had approximately $98.8 million in expenses related to

governmental activities; of which $17.8 million of these expenses were offset by program specific charges for services or grants and contributions. General revenues of $84.9 million were adequate to provide for the remaining costs of these programs.

- Among major funds, the General Fund had $65.5 million in fiscal year 2002 revenues, which primarily consisted of state aid and property taxes, and $65.9 million in expenditures. The General Fund's fund balance decrease from $4.8 million as of June 30, 2001, to $4.2 million as of June 30, 2002, was primarily due to an additional health insurance premium assessment during the current fiscal year.
- The District's total bonded debt decreased $3.4 million during the current fiscal year due to retirement of school improvement and refunding bonds.
- The District defeased $20,365,000 of outstanding School Improvement Bonds by issuing $21,570,000 in refunding bonds to reduce total debt service payments over the next 13 years by $583,500.

OVERVIEW OF FINANCIAL STATEMENTS

This discussion and analysis are intended to serve as an introduction to the District's basic financial statements. The District's basic financial statements comprise three components: 1) government-wide financial statements, 2) fund financial statements, and 3) notes to the financial statements. This report also contains other supplementary information in addition to the basic financial statements themselves.

Government-wide financial statements. The government-wide financial statements are designed to provide readers with a broad overview of the District's finances, in a manner similar to a private-sector business.

The statement of net assets presents information on all of the District's assets and liabilities, with the difference between the two reported as net assets. Over time, increases or decreases in net assets may serve as a useful indicator of whether the financial position of the District is improving or deteriorating.

The statement of activities presents information showing how the District's net assets changed during the most recent fiscal year. All changes in net assets are reported as soon as the underlying event giving rise to the change occurs, regardless of the timing of related cash flows. Thus, revenues and expenses are reported in this statement for some items that will only result in cash flows in future fiscal periods (e.g., uncollected taxes and earned but unused compensated absences).

The government-wide financial statements outline functions of the District that are principally supported by property taxes and intergovernmental revenues. The governmental activities of the District include instruction, support services, operation and maintenance of plant, student transportation, operation of non-instructional services, and interest on long-term debt.

The government-wide financial statements can be found on pages 18 and 19 of this report.

Fund financial statements. A fund is a grouping of related accounts that is used to maintain control over resources that have been segregated for specific activities or objectives. The District uses fund accounting to ensure and demonstrate compliance with finance-related legal requirements. All of the funds of the District can be divided into two categories: governmental funds and fiduciary funds.

Governmental funds. Governmental funds are used to account for essentially the same functions reported as governmental activities in the government-wide financial statements. However, unlike the government-wide financial statements, governmental fund financial statements focus on near-term inflows of spendable resources, as well as on balances of spendable resources available at the end of the fiscal year. Such information may be useful in evaluating the District's near-term financing requirements.

Because the focus of governmental funds is narrower than that of the government-wide financial statements, it is useful to compare the information presented for governmental funds with similar information presented for governmental activities in the government-wide financial statements. By doing so, readers may better understand the long-term impact of the District's near-term financing decisions. Both the governmental fund balance sheet and the governmental fund statement of revenues, expenditures, and changes in fund balances provide a reconciliation to facilitate this comparison between governmental funds and governmental activities. These reconciliations are on pages 24 and 28, respectively.

In accordance with Arizona Revised Statutes (A.R.S.), the District maintains forty-four individual governmental funds. Information is presented separately in the governmental fund balance sheet and in the governmental fund statement of revenues, expenditures, and changes in fund balances for the General and Debt Service Funds, both of which are considered to be major funds. Data from the other forty-two governmental funds are combined into a single, aggregated presentation. Individual fund data for each of these non-major governmental funds is provided in the form of combining statements and schedules beginning on page 58 of this report.

The basic governmental fund financial statements can be found on pages 22 through 28 of this report.

Fiduciary funds. Fiduciary funds are used to account for resources held for the benefit of parties outside the District. Fiduciary funds are not reflected in the government-wide financial statements because the resources of those funds are not available to support the District's own programs. The accrual basis of accounting is used for fiduciary funds.

The basic fiduciary fund financial statement can be found on page 29 of this report.

Notes to the financial statements. The notes provide additional information that is essential to a full understanding of the data provided in the government-wide and fund financial statements. The notes to the financial statements can be found on pages 30 through 47 of this report.

Other information. In addition to the basic financial statements and accompanying notes, this report also presents certain required supplementary information concerning the District's budget process. The District adopts an annual expenditure budget for all governmental funds. A budgetary comparison schedule has been provided for the General Fund as required supplementary information. This required supplementary information can be found on pages 49 through 50 of this report.

The combining statements referred to earlier in connection with non-major governmental funds are presented immediately following the required supplementary information on budgets. Combining and individual fund statements and schedules can be found on pages 55 through 122 of this report.

GOVERNMENT-WIDE FINANCIAL ANALYSIS

Net assets may serve over time as a useful indicator of a government's financial position. In the case of the District, assets exceeded liabilities by $51,042,036 as of June 30, 2002.

By far the largest portion of the District's net assets (50.6 percent) reflects its investment in capital assets (e.g., land and improvements, buildings and improvements, vehicles, furniture and equipment, and construction in progress), less any related debt used to acquire those assets that is still outstanding. The District uses these capital assets to provide services to its students; consequently, these assets are not available for future spending. Although the District's investment in its capital assets is reported net of related debt, it should be noted that the resources needed to repay this debt must be provided from other sources, since the capital assets themselves cannot be used to liquidate these liabilities.

The District's financial position is the product of several financial transactions including the net results of activities, the acquisition and payment of debt, the acquisition and disposal of capital assets, and the depreciation of capital assets.

Figure B-1 presents a summary of the District's net assets for the fiscal years ended June 30, 2002 and 2001, respectively. The following are sig-

Figure B-1   Summary of the District's Net Assets for 2002 and 2001.

	As of June 30, 2002	As of June 30, 2001
Current assets	$ 36,796,160	$ 34,436,268
Deferred charges	1,109,578	
Capital assets	87,992,321	87,368,554
Total assets	125,898,059	121,804,822
Current liabilities	14,383,966	11,175,977
Long-term debt outstanding	60,472,057	64,097,450
Total liabilities	74,856,023	75,273,427
Net assets:		
Invested in capital assets, net of related debt	25,835,394	19,133,554
Restricted	9,161,468	16,636,056
Unrestricted	16,045,174	10,761,785
Total net assets	$ 51,042,036	$ 46,531,395

nificant current year transactions that have had an impact on the Statement of Net Assets.

- The principal retirement of $4,620,000 of school improvement and refunding bonds.
- The addition of $3.9 million in capital assets through the construction of new schools and other school improvements and purchases of furniture, equipment and vehicles.
- Claims and judgments payable amounting to $1,410,364 resulting from an additional health insurance premium assessment.
- The issuance of $21,570,000 in refunding bonds to advance refund $20,365,000 of outstanding school improvement bonds.

Changes in net assets. The District's total revenues for the fiscal year ended June 30, 2002, were $102.7 million. The total cost of all programs and services was $98.8 million. Figure B-2 presents a summary of the changes in net assets for the fiscal year ended June 30, 2002 and 2001, respectively.

Governmental activities. Figure B-3 presents the cost of the seven major District functional activities: instruction, support services—

Figure B-2   Summary of the Changes in Net Assets for 2002 and 2001.

	Fiscal year ended June 30, 2002	Fiscal year ended June 30, 2001
Revenues:		
Program revenues:		
Charges for services	$ 2,341,624	$ 2,547,538
Operating grants and contributions	14,713,708	12,050,412
Capital grants and contributions	717,763	412,718
General revenues:		
Property taxes	26,016,624	25,580,793
Investment income	669,025	1,267,843
County aid	3,238,562	3,019,625
State aid	54,982,997	50,520,648
Federal aid	8,731	3,180
Total revenues	102,689,034	95,402,757
Expenses:		
Instruction	55,821,701	49,306,014
Support services – students and staff	10,870,068	10,913,342
Support services – administration	8,216,299	8,036,496
Operations and maintenance of plant services	11,183,891	10,798,392
Student transportation services	2,685,021	2,369,576
Operation of non-instructional services	6,500,270	5,503,797
Interest on long-term debt	3,516,301	3,985,910
Total expenses	98,793,551	90,913,527
Increase in net assets	$ 3,895,483	$ 4,489,230

Figure B-3   Cost of Seven Major District Functional Activities and Each Function's Net
Cost.

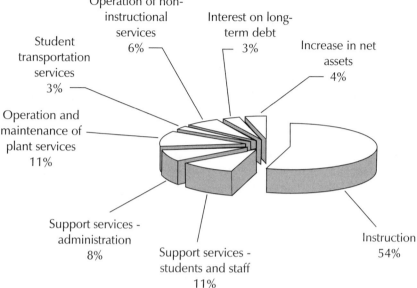

students and staff, support services—administration, operation and maintenance of plant services, student transportation services, operation of
non-instructional services, and interest on long-term debt. The table also
shows each function's net cost (total cost less charges for services generated by the activities and intergovernmental aid provided for specific programs). The net cost shows the financial burden that was placed on the
State and District's taxpayers by each of these functions.

- The cost of all governmental activities this year was $98.8 million.
- The Federal and State governments subsidized certain programs with
  grants and contributions of $15.4 million and fees and other revenues
  subsidized certain activities with charges for services of $2.3 mil-
  lion.
- The net cost of governmental activities of $81.0 million was financed
  by general revenues, which are made up primarily of $26.0 million in
  property taxes, State and County aid of $58.2 million and investment
  income of $669,025.

FINANCIAL ANALYSIS OF
THE DISTRICT'S FUNDS

As noted earlier, the District uses fund accounting to ensure and demonstrate compliance with finance-related legal requirements.

Governmental funds. The focus of the District's governmental funds is to provide information on near-term inflows, outflows, and balances of spendable resources. Such information is useful in assessing the District's financing requirements. In particular, unreserved fund balance may serve as a useful measure of the District's net resources available for spending at the end of the fiscal year.

The financial performance of the District as a whole is reflected in its governmental funds. As the District completed the year, its governmental funds reported a combined fund balance of $19.6 million, a decrease of $2.0 million due primarily to an overall increase in current expenditures resulting from increased payroll and employee benefit costs needed to sustain salary levels competitive with other districts in the state. Approximately $18.9 million, or 96.0 percent of the fund balance constitutes unreserved fund balance. The remaining fund balance of $788,330 is reserved for inventory to indicate that it is not available for spending because it has already been committed.

The General Fund is the principal operating fund of the District. The decrease in fund balance of $594,276 in the General Fund to $4,181,531 was a result of increased expenditures for instruction resulting from certified staff raises and the additional health insurance premium assessment. The Debt Service Fund fund balance showed an insignificant increase of $41,114 from $1,059,585 as of June 30, 2001, to $1,100,699 as of June 30, 2002. The remaining non-major governmental funds showed a fund balance decrease of approximately $1.4 million was primarily the result of the utilization of fund balance for capital improvements in the Bond Building Fund.

BUDGETARY HIGHLIGHTS

The budget variance of $6,198,480 for property tax revenues in the General Fund was primarily a result of using a projected beginning fund balance of $1.5 million. The actual beginning fund balance was $3.5 million. The difference between the budgeted and actual beginning fund balance resulted in a reduced property tax rate for the District and therefore less revenues were collected. The revenue budget was not revised to reflect the change.

Over the course of the year, the District revised the General Fund annual expenditure budget for changes in student population and projected expenditures. Differences between the original budget and the final amended budget were relatively minor. The $1,608,537 increase can be briefly summarized as follows:

- $1,111,350 in increases allocated to regular education in the General Fund.
- $497,187 in increases allocated to special education in the General Fund.

The expenditure budget variance of $2.2 million in the regular education in the General Fund was a result of an increase in budgeted expenditures due to unexpected growth in enrollment for the fiscal year. However, actual expenditures did not increase at the same rate as budgeted expenditures.

A schedule showing the original and final budget amounts compared to the District's actual financial activity for the General Fund is provided in this report as required supplementary information.

Additional information regarding the District's budget process may be found in Note 2 on pages 36 through 37.

CAPITAL ASSETS AND DEBT ADMINISTRATION

Capital Assets. As of June 30, 2002, the District had invested $127.3 million in capital assets, including school buildings, athletic facilities, buses and other vehicles, computers, and other equipment. This amount represents a net increase prior to depreciation of $3.9 million from last year, primarily due to improvements to existing facilities. Total depreciation expense for the year was $3.3 million.

The schedule shown in Figure B-4 presents capital asset balances net of depreciation for the fiscal year ended June 30, 2002, and June 30, 2001. Additional information on the District's capital assets can be found in Note 6 on page 40 of this report.

Debt Administration. At year-end, the District had $64.8 million in general obligation and refunding bonds, of which $4.7 million is due within one year. Figure B-5 presents a summary of the District's outstanding long-term debt for the fiscal year ended June 30, 2002, and June 30, 2001. The District maintains an "AAA" rating from Standard & Poor's and Fitch and an "Aaa" rating from Moody's for general obligation debt.

State statutes currently limit the amount of general obligation debt a District may issue to 30 percent of its total assessed secondary valuation. The current debt limitation for the District is $78,910,021, which is more than the District's outstanding general obligation debt.

Additional information on the District's long-term debt can be found in Notes 7 through 9 on pages 41 through 44 of this report.

During the year ended June 30, 2002, the District issued $21,570,000 in refunding bonds, with an effective interest rate of 4.27 percent, to advance refund $20,365,000 of outstanding general obligation bonds, with an average interest rate of 5.53 percent. This advance refunding was undertaken to reduce the total debt service payments over the next 13 years by $583,500 and resulted in an economic gain of $465,826.

ECONOMIC FACTORS AND NEXT YEAR'S BUDGET AND RATES

Many factors were considered by the District's administration during the process of developing the fiscal year 2002–2003 budget. Among them:

Figure B-4   Capital Asset Balances Net of Depreciation for 2002 and 2001.

	As of June 30, 2002	As of June 30, 2001
Land and improvements	$ 8,648,883	$ 8,495,416
Buildings and improvements	72,273,180	70,254,698
Vehicles, furniture and equipment	6,421,114	6,675,996
Construction in progress	649,144	1,942,444
Total	$87,992,321	$87,368,554

Figure B-5   District's Outstanding Long-Term Debt for 2002 and 2001.

	As of June 30, 2002	As of June 30, 2001
School improvement bonds	$43,250,000	$65,710,000
Refunding bonds	21,570,000	2,525,000
Total	**$64,820,000**	**$68,235,000**

- 2001–02 budget balance carryforward (est. $1.15 million).
- Proposition 301 revenues, carryforward, and limitations (est. $5.3 million).
- District student population (est. 2 percent increase).
- Attrition savings from retirements (est. $400,000).
- Employee salaries (certified, classified and administrative increases from M&O budget).
- Increased cost of health insurance due to the 2002–2003 assessment, by Arizona School Care, the District's health insurance program. Claims expenses were in excess of premiums collected by an estimated $1,410,364.
- Alternative sources of revenues (Medicaid reimbursement).
- Cost cutting measures to improve efficiency and effectiveness of District instructional and non-instructional programs.

Also considered in the development of the budget was the local economy and inflation of the surrounding metropolitan area.

These indicators were considered when adopting the budget for fiscal year 2002–2003. Amounts available in the General Fund budget are $70,339,708, an increase of $2,149,521 (3.2 percent) over the previous year's budget and an increase of $6,209,438 (9.6 percent) over the previous year's actual expenditures. Increased payroll and employee benefit costs are the primary reasons for the increase. Each continuing teacher's 2002–2003 contract was increased by $1,930. This amount included the $630 increase in health insurance premiums per employee. Total estimated cost increase is $1,872,000. Classified employees received $630 increase to salary to cover increased cost of health insurance. $300,000 was also allotted to address reclassification implementation and market study analysis. Administrators received a 4.94 percent increase to salaries. This amount included the $630 increase in health insurance premiums per employee. No new programs were added to the 2002–2003 budget. However, approximately 30 additional classroom teachers were hired to reduce and maintain class size.

CONTACTING THE DISTRICT'S
FINANCIAL MANAGEMENT

This financial report is designed to provide our citizens, taxpayers, and investors and creditors with a general overview of the District's finances and to demonstrate the District's accountability for the resources it receives. If you have questions about this report or need additional information, contact the Business and Finance Department, Sunnyside Unified School District No. 12, 2238 E. Ginter Road, Tucson, Arizona, 85734.

Appendix C

The ASBO Certificate of Excellence in Financial Reporting Program

The Certificate of Excellence in Financial Reporting Program was designed by the Association of School Business Officials (ASBO) International to encourage excellence in the preparation and issuance of school district Comprehensive Annual Financial Reports (CAFRs). A Certificate of Excellence is awarded to school districts that have submitted their CAFR and, upon completion of a technical review, are judged by the review panel members to have satisfied the criteria for excellence in financial reporting. The Certificate of Excellence Award is the highest form of recognition in school financial reporting issued by ASBO International.

The COE Program was established in 1972 and currently receives applications from more than 400 school districts and community-supported educational institutions located throughout the United States. Since Certificates are granted based on a particular fiscal year's report, a school district must resubmit its CAFR annually to maintain its Certificate.

BENEFITS TO PARTICIPANTS IN THE CERTIFICATE OF EXCELLENCE PROGRAM

Prestigious National Award

Since its inception, the program has gained the distinction of being a prestigious national award recognized by:

- Accounting Professionals
- Bond Counsels
- Underwriters
- Securities Analysts
- Educational, Teacher and Citizen Groups
- Federal and State Agencies

Validates Fiscal Credibility

Receipt of a Certificate of Excellence validates a school district's fiscal and financial management credibility with its various reporting constituencies, including:

- School Board Members, Superintendents
- School District Management
- State and Local Government Agencies
- Oversight Entities
- State and Federal Granting Agencies
- Education, Taxpayer and Teacher Organizations

Enhances Report Presentations

Inclusion of a Certificate of Excellence enhances a school district's financial presentations in:

- Annual Reports
- Bond Issuance Official Statements
- Presentations to the Media
- Budget Presentations and Hearings
- Continuing Disclosure Requirements

A Measure of Uniformity

Adherence to the formatting and terminology as promulgated by the appropriate standard setting bodies (GASB, AICPA, etc.) allows for comparability between:

- School districts
- School district reports from year to year

Individual Recognition and Development

Receipt of a Certificate of Excellence provides a school district's board and superintendent with a measure of the integrity and technical competence of the system's fiscal administration. Participation in this landmark program is an unparalleled professional experience.

SUBMITTING A CAFR FOR REVIEW

Participating school districts submit their CAFR and application materials within six months of their fiscal year end. The application must include:

- One copy of the Official Certificate of Excellence Application Form
- Three copies of the school district's CAFR
- Three copies of the school district's responses to the prior year's comments (if applicable)
- Three copies of the Self-Evaluation Worksheet (Submitting the worksheet is optional for school districts that received the award for the prior fiscal year. New applicants, past conditional awards, and past denials are required to complete and submit three copies of the worksheet.)
- Payment based on the total revenue of all funds

Send application, with materials and payment, to: ASBO International, Certificate of Excellence Program, 11401 North Shore Drive, Reston, VA 20190-4200.

To request program information and application materials, contact ASBO International, 11401 North Shore Drive, Reston, VA 20190-4200 / Phone: (703) 478-0405 / Fax: (703) 478-0205 / Website: www.asbointl.org.